the OFFICE

A SURVIVAL GUIDE

▶ Jo Hoare

the OFFICE

A SURVIVAL GUIDE

▶ Jo Hoare

DOG 'n' BONE

Published in 2015 by
Dog 'n' Bone Books

An imprint of

Ryland Peters & Small Ltd.

20–21 Jockey's Fields
London WC1R 4BW

and

341 E 116th St
New York, NY 10029

www.rylandpeters.com

10 9 8 7 6 5 4 3

Text © Jo Hoare 2015
Design and illustration
© Dog 'n' Bone Books 2015

A CIP catalog record for this book
is available from the Library of
Congress and the British Library.

ISBN: 978 1 909313 76 7

Printed in China

Designer: Paul Tilby
Editor: Emma Hill
Illustrator: Paul Parker
Commissioning editor: Pete Jorgensen
Art director: Sally Powell
Production controller: David Hearn
Publishing manager: Penny Craig
Publisher: Cindy Richards

CONTENTS ◀▶

The Book

INTRODUCTION

What did you think you'd be when you grew up? A superhero? Football star? Dinosaur veterinarian? Someone who sat within three square foot of space, encased by cushioned MDF, trying to encourage people to up their monthly spend on photocopier toner?

One of life's saddest facts is that the 99.9% of us who aren't Paris Hilton or Prince William are going to have to be in paid employment for pretty much most of our waking hours until we're too old to do anything decent with that time anyway. For most of us that paid employment will involve sitting in an office.

Ah the office; a sort of night-release prison where you're enslaved between the hours of 9am to 5pm with no choice of who shares your bunk or bathroom, and there's always the underlying feeling someone might shank you with a homemade weapon. You're going to need your wits about you to survive. From identifying and managing the diaspora of freaks 'n' geeks around you to successfully negotiating the horror that is the Christmas party, this book is here to help you. Even if it's only something for you to read in the bathroom while you hide from your boss...

CHAPTER 1

YOUR
COLLEAGUES

Identifiable by her plaintive cries of "Who's been using my soy/cashew/almond milk?" (Ummm, no one, love, it makes coffee taste like it's already been drunk and excreted.) No dairy/carbs/additives/fun have passed her lips since the mid-nineties and her extreme gastro habits affect everyone around her. (Note: We're saying "her," but men are not excluded from this annoying sub genre.)

The Diet Bore begins her day by hogging the kitchen to make her morning porridge using lukewarm water. Apparently, cold water burns more calories and she's saving her soy milk rations for the half dozen appetite-suppressing coffees she'll intersperse the afternoon with. When she's finished pushing her food around with a spoon, she leaves the half-eaten bowl of wallpaper paste by the fridge, unwashed. Within minutes, the mush sets like concrete, thus rendering the bowl useless to anyone without a full archaeological excavation kit tucked under the sink next to the dishwashing liquid.

Next up in her daily routine is the complicated process of blocking the sink with coagulated "lean green" juice. Her Nutribullet couldn't quite deal with the sheer volume of kale she expected it to blend, so lumps of vegetables the same shade as bronchial phlegm sit in the plughole until the mythical man from the facilities department arrives with a plunger that you suspect he also uses for unblocking the toilets.

After The Diet Bore has downed her juice and suppressed the urge to vomit it straight back up again, co-workers get an hour or two of respite until lunchtime, when she uses the microwave to steam some fish. Chances are, unless you lost your sense of smell as a result of a freak head injury, you're going to need to vacate the building before (and apologies to sensitive readers; there's no nice way to put this) any passing blind person could mistake your office for an industrial-sized sanitary bin that is way overdue for emptying.

The Diet Bore

Once she's finished her chemical weapon of a lunch and your eyes have stopped watering, you'd think you might get a chance to enjoy your own food. No way. Her hybrid emotions of envy and horror at your normal-person meal choice do not make for easy digestion. As you rush through your ham and cheese sandwich and slice of cake, feeling guilty and wondering if just the one pair of Spanx might get you back into that dress this weekend, you're ALMOST tempted round to her way of thinking...

Let's be honest, unless you've recently given birth/been at the business end of your partner as she did, you probably have a sneaking suspicion that maternity leave is a bit of a doss. A year off work you say? Hanging out watching cartoons and clogging up Starbucks with your buggy while the rest of us do the work that our company is too tight to pay a replacement you to do? Sounds alright to us... Of course, we know that's not really the case, but it doesn't mean you don't need advice on how to deal with the recently post partum in your worksphere.

THE NOTHING'S GONNA CHANGE POWER MOM

Back in her size-eight suit two weeks after giving birth, she barely noticed the labor process, necking fewer painkillers than you do for a mild mid-week hangover. She was answering emails during contractions, took less time off for mat leave than some people would for the removal of a wisdom tooth, and runs her childcare regime with less flexibility than Kim Jong Il's hairdresser.

HOW TO WIN HER OVER: Subtly bring up other moms in the office who commit heinous, non-power-mom crimes, such as occasionally seeing their offspring in daylight or cluttering up their desks with ostentatious snaps of their kids. Hearing that Clare was seven minutes late after a tricky school run, or Amy's taken a half day due to an outbreak of chicken pox, will delight her more than seeing her firstborn's first steps.

THE "I SEE THE WORLD WITH RENEWED EYES" MOM

She didn't have a baby—she had a magical blessing. She's not a woman—she's a fertile goddess. And you already have a headache from listening to it. Dismissing her previous life of scamming cocktails on expenses and getting off with sales reps at conferences, she now pities anyone who cares for such shallow life frivolities as hair brushing or talking in full adult English.

HOW TO WIN HER OVER: Stick it out for a little while—lack of sleep tends to have an adverse effect on one's general sense of awe and wonder at creating new life. If it hasn't faded after a few months, leave leaflets around for training courses in holistic aromatherapy midwifery. She'll be off quicker than you can say pan-fried placenta.

THE RELUCTANT RETURNER

Pre-baby you may very well have gotten on like the proverbial incandescent abode, but now the thing she hates most in the world is keeping her away from the thing she loves most. And whereas you don't blame her, all that chat about the varying shades of fecal matter in her child's diaper is putting you off your green juice, and your level of knowledge about her healing perineum is something that's beginning to haunt your dreams. Plus, if she's late every day because of another binky/blanket/breast pump incident, who's going to cover your back when you need that extra half hour duvet time?

HOW TO WIN HER OVER: Your first thought will be to pretend to be interested, but it's a very dangerous game; you'll start with gateway pleasantries like cooing over iPhone pictures and asking after their night's sleep and soon your life will become a living, breathing Mumsnet forum. And nobody wants that. The alternative? Well, short of pretending you've recently shacked up with a convicted sex offender, there's only one answer in a case like this. Headphones. Massive, great, noise-canceling ones like Blue Ivy wears backstage. And wear them 'til the kid hits 18.

When entering a new workplace it's tempting to take the magpie approach to new friends, and no one is as eye-catchingly shiny to the office newbie than The Party Animal. Whether it's the dipped-in-Touche-Éclat-foundation, wine pomander party girl or the Bantersauraus Rex, wisecracking party boy, both are at first glance your best bet for office matedom. Treat them with caution, though, as a wrong move could see both your liver and livelihood heading for failure.

THE PERMA HANGOVER

With a desk never featuring less than five different types of liquid refreshment, you can judge the level of the Perma Hangover's pain by their choice of drink. Full fat coke before 9am? Do not approach. Delicate sips from a Red Bull can? Definitely don't sit between them and the door in your early morning meeting. Black coffee? You might get some work from them around 11am. Getting into the lift with them first thing would make you fail a breathalyzer test, so save evenings out with them for when you've got the next day off.

USEFUL BECAUSE: Their desk drawer could keep Dr. House in painkillers for a month, so make them your office pharmacy.

THE LAD

Not quite sure how to identify the party Lad? Look down. No, a bit further than that. What's that you see around his ankle region? Is it a hint of a comedy sock! Something bright and anti-establishment with maybe a humorously misspelt cartoon character... "Boner Simpson" anyone? Because, although the bosses can make him wear a suit, that inch of shoe to lower shin can't be contained by corporate big boys! Congratulations, you've found him! Able to spend 90% of his wages on drinks that come in some kind of treasure chest because he still lives at home with his parents, if a night out doesn't end in the reappearance of the aforementioned chest-encased booze (probably all over your shoes), it's been disappointing. Fond of using "humorous" clip art in his presentations, writing rude messages in office birthday cards, and trying to saddle everyone in the workplace with one of his hilarious nicknames. If you're not a member of a sports team or on your university year in industry placement, you might want to steer clear.

The Party Animal

USEFUL BECAUSE: Got a score to settle in the office? He's your perfect revenge envoy. Fill him up with booze and plonk him down next to the office bitch. And her brand new handbag.

THE PAST-IT PARTY GIRL

Apparently, she was quite the face sometime in the early 1990s (for this read, she once waited in line for the toilet next to a Spice Girl) and she's never really got over it. Nowadays, it takes quite the maintenance program to keep up with the young ones' after-work boozing, but with a careful regime of vitamin pills, juice cleanses, and the occasional trip to Dr. B. Tox she's just about getting away with it. Schooled in the art of office boozing back in the day where lunches lasted until 7pm and work dinners came with a compulsory course of narcotics, she will be able to drink more than anyone else you work with. So bear that in mind before challenging her.

USEFUL BECAUSE: She can probably expense the drinks.

THE PARTY FAKER

This is a dangerous subsection and a lot more common than you think. The Party Faker always says yes to Friday drinks, birthday do's, and any other occasion where the booze will be flowing, but keep an eye on their glass... while they're merrily offering you your seventh top up of the evening, and you're thinking they're along for the ride (admittedly one in a vomit comet), they've been nursing the same drink for hours and are just biding their time for their stealth social media takedown of everyone foolish enough not to bust their planned sobriety. The favored modus operandi of a Faker is to act as unofficial night photographer snapping away at all the flirting/bitching/falling over that occurs and then combine this with the most unflattering angles and poses before packaging it all up as a neat little Facebook album. The Party Faker then posts the incriminating pics online the next morning, a good three hours before anyone who actually drank their drinks will resurface. This ensures that when you do log on to de-tag the picture where your gusset is exposed to the room, the one where you look like you have 13 chins, or a trick of the light that appears to show you fondling Dave in accounts, the whole world has already seen them anyway.

USEFUL BECAUSE: A minefield of blackmailable info, make friends with him and he'll tell you everything about everyone. Plus you might be able to veto that picture of you playing cock or ball with the intern.

With everyone being more or less aware that out-and-out sexual harassment is generally frowned upon, the workplace perving of yesteryear is largely absent from most offices. That's not to say there isn't still the odd archetypal, slimy bastard yelling "while you're down there" every time you drop something on the floor and accidentally-on-purpose grinding their groin against you when they make their way to the photocopier but, by and large, the office sex pest has had to dial down their overt creep-ness. This doesn't mean you're any safer though... there's simply a new breed of sleaze on the loose. Be warned. Be aware.

THE TOUCHY FEELER

Fifteen years ago he'd have been patting your bottom when you were a "good girl" but the modern day TF has had to work on a subtler modus operandi. The elbow to side boob graze in a busy elevator? No accident. The guiding hand on the small of your back through a door? Lining up the perfect vantage point for ogling your bottom. You probably think he's sweet and harmless. He's probably married. But give him three beers on a night out and he'll be trying to undo your bra through your blouse before passing out in your lap.

THE OGLER

Remember "sticks and stones can break my bones but words can never hurt me?" Well, The Ogler has repurposed that: "Touches and feels can break my disciplinary record but looking can never hurt me." Like a grown-up, creepy version of your kid brother hovering his hand an inch above you while saying "I'm not touching you," with this guy you can't go running to mom/HR because he hasn't actually done anything.

THE HIGH ON HRT AKA THE MENOPAUSAL (SEX) MANIAC

The Office Perv

An increasingly common sub-type of office perv, the fifty-something lady letch means the dirty old woman has taken center stage. The kids have gone to college and hubby's laid up with a suspected hernia, so Sue is flying high on a potent cocktail of freedom, frustration, and a lot of artificial hormones. Having turned her son's bedroom into a gym (also explains away the hernia), she's shed the pounds, read an article in *Good Housekeeping* about how to be a cougar, flicked her way (no pun intended) through E.L. James, and firmly believes that 50 is most definitely the new 30. You'll find her talking loudly about her new bedroom toys with the "girls" (other women in their 50s and 60s), making lewd sexual innuendo about everything from your lunch choices to your new tie, and extolling the virtues of sex (or rumpy pumpy as she probably calls it) as a menopause symptom cure-all.

THE ONE WHO CLAIMS CREDIT

A baffling creature, the Credit Claimer can frequently be both the cleverest and the stupidest person in your office and, as such, is a very tricky character to deal with.

Just like the Inuits have 57 words for snow (ok, we know that's a myth but you get the point), their scamming is so proficient that often they've created a whole nonsensical vocabulary devoted to masking the fact that they've really been sitting on their ass all day choosing which snacks to fill their Graze boxes with, or sourcing shabby chic signs on eBay. Here's what to watch out for:

"THAT'S IN LINE WITH WHAT I'VE BEEN HEARING"

The Credit Claimer will punctuate anyone else's offerings of new information with the above. They want you to think that whatever you have to bring to the table, they've already cut it up, scoffed it down, and put the leftovers in the fridge for tomorrow. No one knows from who, where, how, or why they've "heard" it all before—maybe their aural skills need to be recruited by search and rescue teams—and, sadly, they say it with such confidence that nobody ever challenges them.

"AS I'VE PREVIOUSLY SAID"

Presumably this mythical "saying" happened at the same time as the unsubstantiated "hearing." This phrase is that bit more useful for the CC, though, as not only can you use it over the top of someone else's hard work: "That report you've been working on for a month, that, as I've previously said, reveals changing three key suppliers would reduce our outgoings by 33%?", they can also use it to cover up things they've forgotten to do: "The background checks on that contract? As I've previously said, I needed you to take another look at that."

The One Who Claims Credit For Everyone Else's Work

"I PUT IN 120% WORK IN 70% OF THE TIME"

Bullshit math is one of the most powerful weapons in The Credit Claimer's arsenal. Seemingly indecipherable equations, often including the mathematically impossible and giving more than 100%, are the quickest and easiest way to make everyone glaze over, as who the hell really has the time (or the ability) to work out if these sums even make sense.

"YOU DON'T KNOW WHAT I'VE BEEN DOING BEHIND THE SCENES ON THIS"

Aha, the land of behind the scenes—trickier than Narnia to access and about as realistic. There's a reason no one knows what the CC has been doing behind the scenes and, until someone invents a unit of measurement equivalent to "absolutely fuck all," it's likely to remain unexplained.

THE MEAN GIRL GANG

Now this title is a little misleading... because this sub-tribe of colleagues actually aren't that mean at all, mainly because they're a little too dim to actually mastermind anything bitchy, and you know picking out coordinating pens to match that day's outfit already takes up 65% of that day's brainpower, so there's not all that much left.

Instead, let's rename the tribe of shiny on the outside, somewhat questionable on the inside, girls who have to be hospitalized with hysteria when one of them gets engaged and for whom emojis are their primary means of communication as the NBD's, Nice-But-Dims.

IDENTIFY YOUR NBD GIRL GANG

How many of the following can you tick off?

1. Has a Michael Kors watch.

2. Brings in own "fancy" stationery from home.

3. Has a schedule of work hairstyles, wavy Monday, topknot Tuesday, sleek Wednesday...

4. Pulls her lunch into teeny tiny bite-size pieces before only eating a quarter of it anyway.

5. Hashtags her boyfriend as #theboy on all social media.

6. Carries stuff to work in battered designer carrier bag.

7. Has her own cutesy coffee cup.

8. Campaigns for lunchtime Pilates classes in your meeting room.

9. Her screensaver is a screenshot of her Pinterest wedding mood board.

10. She answers the phone in a baby voice.

11. Her make-up bag sits on her desk at all times.

12. Is one of the last people on earth to still think cupcakes are "cute."

13. Isn't aware the camera on her phone can also be turned outward... to actually take pictures of other people? But why would you do that?

14. Has a scented candle next to her phone.

15. Wears jangly bangles that clank annoyingly as she types.

16. Has a special ringtone for mom.

RESULTS

Tally up your score to see how you did.

The Mean Girl Gang

0–4 Maybe give them the benefit of the doubt, perhaps she just has friends with poor taste who buy her NBD-style gifts and she's too polite not to use them.

5–8 You might need to do further investigations. Show her one of those photos of a random baby in a flowerpot. If she likes it, you know.

MORE THAN 8 Give them a wide berth. Until you need to borrow a tampon—they'll have a whole drawer of feminine hygiene for all occasions.

Coming in only two varieties, the modern-day interns sit at points on the capability spectrum as far apart as JenAn and Angelina are kept from each other on the red carpet.

At the one end we have the super-keen whizz kid who could (and probably will) step into your job tomorrow. And at the other? The person who at regular times of the day you go and hold a mirror under their nostrils to check they're still breathing. Neither the show-you-up whippersnapper nor the dead behind the eyes are what you want in an assistant, but there are no half measures in the intern game. For some reason, Generation 00 has bred only extreme personalities and, unfortunately, your workplace will soon be overrun with them. Below are hints on dealing with some of The Intern's most irritating characteristics.

TYPE ONE: DEAD BEHIND THE EYES

THE PROBLEM: Considers the time it takes her to change from her commuter running shoes into her office heels as part of her working day and thus factors it in as something needing to happen 10 minutes before home time. And it does take her 10 minutes. To do each shoe.

HOW TO DEAL WITH IT: Send her to do something that very much requires the wearing of shoes, be it sweeping of broken glass, gathering of stinging nettles etc. Be sure to set this task 15 minutes before the end of the day.

THE PROBLEM: Has never spoken on the phone. Ever. To anyone. And looks at the phone on her desk the same way someone with a nervous tic might eye up a nuclear reactor red button.

HOW TO DEAL WITH IT: Superglue.

THE PROBLEM: You have spoken more to her parents than her as they ring constantly to ask when you're giving her a job, or to call in sick because she's sprained an ankle (presumably while changing her aforementioned shoes).

HOW TO DEAL WITH IT: Play them at their own game. Call them back pretending to be your mother or father (making sure your impression of your parent involves an extremely cantankerous, hard-of-hearing person).

TYPE TWO: WHIPPERSNAPPER

The Intern

THE PROBLEM: As a member of Generation Post-Facebook, he thinks mainstream social media is for his grandmother, and you're sure he's trying to catch you out by pretending he's on a new absent-voweled "intrnt" site every day.

HOW TO DEAL WITH IT: Try making up one of your own to catch her out. "What do you mean Happn? I heard that was over, everyone's on Xstnce nowadays."

THE PROBLEM: Already earning more than you, thanks to the blog/micro scooter importation business/boutique digital consultancy he set up when he was 13.

HOW TO DEAL WITH IT: At least you're not a virgin, hey.

25

Like the worst ever roommate you had at university, the office Pedant loves nothing more than a sniffy note left on the fridge/meeting-room door/perpetrator's forehead.

No office misdemeanor is too small for them to get their undies into a considerable knot over. Complaining about everything, from the amount of toilet paper being used per day—the system simply can't cope with it—to people allowing microscopic crumbs from their birthday cakes to fall within a five-foot radius of her cubicle. Thinly veiled threats to their colleagues are what make their days worth living. In real life The Pedant is somewhat elusive, fearful of face-to-face confrontation, passive aggressiveness is their usual modus operandi, and they live a shadowy existence, often enhanced by their natural habitat of basement office dwelling.

Probably the kind of person who considers consumer complaints one of their hobbies and knows more about the rights of the customer than most legal professionals, the pass-agg Pedant is frequently found in the twin F professions of finance and facilities. If they're one of the former, they'll treat every penny of the company's money as their own and launch a full-scale investigation into the tax implications of a charity bake sale.

The latter? They'll expect as much notice for the booking of a meeting room as you'd have to give to enter Bhutan. And don't even think about leaving the leftovers from the conference sandwich platter for the rest of the office to enjoy; she'll find at least seven health and safety rules you're breaking and will very likely campaign for your instant dismissal.

The Pedant

If all that doesn't rile you enough, then there's something else you should know about The Pedant—they're definitely being treated much better than you. Why? Well consider the following: Do you have any idea where your employment contract is right now? Of course you don't, you signed it in a haze of relief when you got the job, CBA to really read it properly, then shoved it into a drawer. Somewhere. Maybe not so much a drawer. Ok, the bin, you probably threw it in the bin. Not so The Pedant—they made multiple copies and stored them away neatly in their home filing cabinet. Right next to their updated job description (they ask for a review every six months, 'cos you know otherwise people might take liberties) and last year's appraisal form. Where they have separate clearly demarcated folders, neatly labeled with their homemade stickers from their Dynamo machine, so if they need that gas bill that overcharged them in 1999 for $7.37, they have it to hand in an instant, and if anyone tries to make them do ANYTHING that's not in their contract? Well they've got a fight on their hands. With their battle cry being "I think you'll find it's not in my job description," it's easier just to do the bloody thing yourself. Pedant 1; You 0.

What you holding out for buddy? A gold carriage clock? Actually, what exactly was it about gold carriage clocks that made them such a popular way of commemorating the fact that some poor sap had given over about 70% of his entire waking life to some awful insurance firm or the like. Ok, we've taken a huge chunk and, to be honest, your best years from you, but now you're on a downward spiral to, at best, minor incontinence, here's something to help you count down those remaining days.

Having started way back when the presentation of a piece of gilt tat was more than adequate retribution for a lifetime's endeavors, it's likely no one has broken it to your office Lifer that these past 40 years will not be culminating in the grand presentation of a travel-appropriate timepiece. A hasty office whip round will pay for the second cheapest bottle of whiskey in the shop across the street, and the goodbye card will be mis-signed by at least three people who thought it was the one for Sue's new baby.

The Lifer

DECEMBER 1973

Don't feel too guilty, though. The Lifer has it made at work and FYI the reason no one's communicated his change of events vis-à-vis chronograph-based gratitude for years served is because they would never dream of striking up a conversation with a "newbie." So, with their channels of information being reduced to fellow Lifers, they're not always terribly up to date. Refusal to consider anyone's opinion who hasn't been in the company long enough to remember the good old days when you could pinch a bottom, call a spade a spade, and create a fog of Marlboro around your desk is only the beginning of the perks of being a lifer. Chances are they're also on a way better contract than you are, having signed up in the heady pre-recession decades when a pay rise wasn't on a par with a confirmed sighting of a Yeti in terms of probability.

This is a dangerous category, and not for the exciting snogging in stairwells/copping off in the copy room reasons you're thinking. Nor is it risky because of the potential sexual harassment issue (because TBH, it's not the 1960s in the offices of Sterling Cooper, we all know how to behave now). The real threat is a far more stealth concern, and one you definitely need to be aware of. Read on and allow us to introduce you to the biggest problem facing workplace crushes...

There are many ways in which office life mirrors your school days and nowhere is this more apparent than with the phenomenon of FFW—Fit For Work. No, this isn't some government initiative to stop people watching Jerry Springer while faking slipped discs, this is an occurrence that happens in every workplace up and down the country where your bored mind casts mirage-like attractiveness over anyone even vaguely normal-looking. Just as any teacher under 30 (in stone and age) became the lust object for a hundred schoolboy/girl fantasies, if Darren from marketing manages to shower most days and has a haircut that doesn't look too much like it happened in a sheep-shearing competition, or Jenny in facilities isn't quite as old as your mum and in certain lights (i.e. none) has a certain look of Kim Cattrall about her, then they've probably already cemented their status as your prime FFW'ers.

Kept in check the risks of FFW are fairly low; the five-minute fantasies during the mind-numbing meeting, the occasional smiley or winky face at the end of an email, pinching someone else's posh coffee when you're making the object of your affections a drink. All of these are perfectly within the boundaries of acceptable FFW behavior, but take it any further at your own risk because FFW is very rarely FIRL (Fit In Real Life).

The One Everyone
Fancies

WHO IS AT THE HIGHEST RISK OF FALLING FOR FFW?

If you like boys, does your office consist mostly of girls or vice versa? If the amount of people ticking your sexual preference list is already horribly low, it stands to reason that your standards will be equally so. Don't agree? Think back to your pre-big-city days (and, yes, for "big city" read anywhere that has stores open past 4pm and you don't know the names of your neighbors) and remember how you thought an instant jar of Nescafé was all the coffee you ever needed? Nowadays you wouldn't be seen dead without a cup of something that has a grander title than most minor European royalty, and almost costs as much to subsidize. Think of your FFW like your Nescafé—it does the job but you probably wouldn't take it out in the street.

AM I AN FFW?

Thought you were quite the catch at work? Get more than your fair share of "banter" from the opposite sex? Had the odd anonymous Valentines card? A saucy Secret Santa gift at Christmas? So far, so good, but hang on a minute, are you an average-looking person in a workplace where the median attractiveness falls somewhere between Piers Morgan and Mama June from *Here Comes Honey Boo Boo*? Does wearing something that's less than 90% polyester mark you out as an office "trendsetter"? Are you alone in having changed your haircut since the last millennium? If you answered yes to any of the above, then, sorry to break it to you, but you may be a classic FFW. If you've attempted to initiate outside-of-work contact (N.B. Work drinks that spill over into another bar don't count; there needs to be a minimum of two non-work friends accompanying the FFW fancier to act as adjudicators) and it has never come to fruition, you're a FFW, Cinderella, and your midnight is 5pm on a Friday till 9am on a Monday.

I THINK MY OFFICE CRUSH IS GENUINELY HOT, HOW DO I TELL?

OCCASIONALLY you might be right. There are recorded cases dating back to the 1980's PDAI (Pre-dating App Invention) where people actually met and married their colleagues! And just maybe your senses haven't been rendered entirely useless from the monotony of spirit-crushing drudgery and you genuinely have spotted a good 'un. If you really think this is the case, just answer the following teeny checklist first...

HAVE YOU EVER SEEN THEM STAND UP? Many's the case of FFW longing that's been crushed in an instant with the simple act of elevation from chair. If you've only gazed at them longingly in meetings, then they arise to be a) a foot shorter than anticipated b) wearing white socks with black shoes c) sporting sweatpants with their shirt and tie in the manner of a newsreader whose top half you're only ever going to see, your FFW crush is going to disappear quicker than wrinkles on a Madonna album cover.

The One Everyone Fancies

HAVE YOU SEEN THEM IN THEIR OUT-OF-WORK CLOTHES? Especially important if you have any kind of uniform or strict dress code in your workplace. For all you know, outside of their 9–5 wardrobe, their downtime dress could be made entirely of fleece/unchanged since 1989/consist only of Nazi historical re-enactment live action role play uniforms (if it's the last, the outfits might kind of be the least of your worries).

HOW MANY DRINKS? Be honest now, if you saw them in a bar, at what point would you find them attractive? Are they a start of the nighter, a somewhat loosened up a third of the way through the evening, a "starting to panic now" hour to go, or a regretful case of a desperate race against the lights coming on? Anything hovering around the panic mark and FFW looms large.

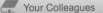
Nothing brings out extremes in the workplace like a bout of office illness. Whereas most of your colleagues will probably have a reasonably sensible view of sickness (and we're talking proper illness, not sickies—for a handle on that see pages 36–37) and run through a checklist of: Can I get out of bed? Do I need to be within five feet of a toilet? Am I liable to collapse if I attempt to board the number 38 bus? Will I be of any use to anyone at all if I do drag myself in? And decide that a positive response to any of the above does indeed merit a duvet day, there are those for whom it's way more complicated than that. Meet The Illness Martyr and The Sicknote. Polar opposites and almost equally annoying in their attitude to workplace health, it's a close-fought battle as to who will piss you off most. Let's hear the case for both:

THE ILLNESS MARTYR

Just like old people can't resist telling you their age at any given opportunity—"I'm 88 you know, dear?" "Umm yeah, you want fries with that?", the most overwhelming accomplishment in The Illness Martyr's life is the years gone without a single sick day. "Seven years, and not a single day off sick," they'll exclaim, beating their chest and looking for a medal. What this statement doesn't take into account is the number of times they've dragged themselves in in various states of mucus/vomit/diarrhea/fever takeover and coughed/sprayed/sneezed/left particles of fecal matter (sorry but its true) all over things you have to then touch, thus making you and yours sick as hell. Thanks a lot.

Not that you'd ever be as sick as them, though. The Illness Martyr is highly competitive and also disgustingly descriptive. Whereas The Sicknote uses exhaustive explanations of their hourly symptoms, both to ward off naysayers and because they consider illness as one of their hobbies, the IM reports on each stage of a sickness as a war cabinet might detail a battle. They won't have slept at all the night before. Their temperature would have been the highest any doctor had ever seen (conversely, The Illness Martyr loves going to the doctor, because a validated illness and still coming in is the ultimate slap in the face to all you wusses who take time off when you can't breathe/see straight/leave the toilet for more than 15 seconds). If you had to take eight painkillers yesterday, they rival Jesse Pinkman in their collection of epinephrine. They'll describe the shades of their phlegm to you with Pantone-esque attention to detail and you'll be lucky enough to hear exactly what state they've just left the bowl of trap three in. But still THEY WON'T GO HOME.

HOW TO DEAL WITH THEM:

DO: Ignore. Ignore. Ignore. That whimper after every hacking cough and the groan after the 347th nose blow are tactics to get you to look up and say those four little words… "you should go home." That is precisely what the IM wants so they can launch into their pre-prepared diatribe about being too busy/important/annoying to do anything so human as be sick.

DON'T: Try to compete. That cold you had at the weekend is most definitely not the same cold as they have now. And the stomach flu that laid you up for a week last winter? Not a patch on the hitherto undiscovered levels of gastric issues they're manfully putting up with right now.

DO: Get wicked. If you're bored and in need of a little entertainment, then talk down every symptom they describe. Your cough? Didn't notice it TBH. You've got a temperature? Well it is very hot in here, maybe the air con has broken. You just regurgitated a lung? Lucky you've got two then. Pretty soon they'll have worked themselves up into a coronary-inducing rage and even an IM's gotta take a day or two off for that.

THE SICKNOTE

The Sicknote has an encyclopedic knowledge of health. Well, what they like to consider an encyclopedic knowledge, that is. In reality, unless Brittanica was rewritten by one of those Nigerian princes that keeps offering you a $2.5 billion stake in his personal fortune should you help him out with a few bank details, it's far from the truth. With all of their knowledge gleaned from watching *Grey's Anatomy* and falling into rabbit warrens of self-diagnosis websites on Google, these are the kind of people who don't really know their scrotum from their sacrum, but are equally concerned about doing a mischief to both.

Likely to have at least three pre-existing complaints—all going by indecipherable acronyms—these various fatigue/skeletal/fungal problems are The Sicknote's stock-in-trade, getting them out of all manner of annoying inconveniences: coming back to work the day after the Christmas holidays; coming back to work on a Monday morning; coming into work at all. When they're actually at work the list of things they can't do is endless: unable to exist without their "special" support chair/ergonomic keyboard/air purifier etc., etc. If you haven't got room in your meeting for a full medical assessment to take place, you might as well forget about it.

Second only to their enjoyment of scamming extra days off due to their pre-existing complaints is their barely disguised glee when a major bug befalls the office. As soon as there's a whisper that Pete down in finance might have been a little loose of stool, they're already ringing the plague bell of norovirus and awaiting their own inevitable descent into a D-and-V-themed minibreak. And as for flu season? It's practically the second coming.

All of this you could probably cope with if it weren't for the fact that they're convinced that you, their unfortunate colleague, is as fascinated by their health as they are. You'll get a blow-by-blow (literally in the case of their latest adenoid infection—hint: It's never just a cold for The Sicknote) of every stage of their latest affliction and become far more familiar with the workings of their digestive tract than you are with your own.

HOW TO DEAL WITH THEM:

DO: Study part time, get a medical degree, then call them out on all of their BS. Long-winded? Yes. But think of how satisfying it'd be.

DON'T: Think that pretending to be ill yourself will scare them off. They'll be hungry for your germs like the mythical backpacker who wanted to get thin in India, so licked her own flip flop. Expect to see them volunteering to wash your coffee cup up or wiping your phone on their face.

DO: Try and call them out. After a long monologue about their symptoms, tell a tale of someone else with an extra erroneous one in there. "Cough, fever, dizziness, what about the appearance of blue hives all over your left knee? That's what Debbie on level six had." Guaranteed, within the hour, they'll be reporting exactly the same.

DON'T: Ever, ever, ever ask "How are you?" The Sicknote doesn't understand the social niceties of this statement as being one rung up from a grunted "hello" and thinks instead it is the chance to spew forth about, well, maybe their spewing.

There are lots of people who make your life hell at work. Some actively go out of their way to do so, others are simply born with the talent, but there's a particular genre of irritating colleague that sits in between these two ends of intent. You're sure they're not deliberately going out of their way to offend you, but neither are they taking the necessary steps to ensure they don't... meet the office Stinker. Every workplace has one, and if you think you don't, it's probably you.

Cast aside the idea that you'll be able to spot the olfactory abuser instantly—The Stinker often hides in plain sight. Looking perfectly presentable means your suspicions will at first be deflected to the guy that always has egg on his tie, or someone who really needs to switch their shampoo brand to the medicated aisle. But no, these unfortunate souls are causing your nasal passages no harm whatsoever. Ignore the visuals and follow your nose... found them yet? You'll know when you do.

At first you'll give them the benefit of the doubt. Maybe the commute that morning was a little more packed than usual, or their hot water isn't working, or they've just run out of deodorant. But as the days mount up, the excuses start running out and so does your patience. As your nine-to-five life basically becomes endless hours spent in an armpit-scented fume cabinet, you're going to have to do something. If second-hand smoke is a crime, passive BO inhalation has got to be equally punishable. But how can you deal with it?

The Stinker

HONESTY IS THE BEST POLICY

Ok that header is already untrue as, honestly, you're very unlikely to take this option. Just like telling someone his flies are undone or she has spinach in her teeth we know it's the kindest thing to do but can you seriously imagine pulling poor Kate in sustainability aside and telling her that her lack of a daily shower is making everyone within a five-foot radius' eyes water? Unlikely isn't the word. N.B. If the perpetrator is male, then in some circumstances the "jokey bantz" BO protocol may be invoked. This consists of another male colleague pointing out his fellow male's unpleasant odor under the guise of some misogynistic horseplay i.e. "Bit hot in here today isn't it mate. Hear some of those chicks have been moaning about how much us boys stink. Best stock up on the Right Guard, right? Bloody women."

MANAGE UP

This is a double win if you also hate your boss. Tell your line manager that it's affecting your productivity and wellbeing, and something needs to be done, then watch them sweat (pun intended) it out as they decide how to tell them. That's why they get paid more than you after all.

MAKE A NOTE

Everyone knows Post-its left on a computer are the slings and arrows of a coward but 'tis better to be lacking courage than lacking personal hygiene.

PLAY DUMB

When is BO not BO? When you're pretending it's something else entirely. For this ploy, identify loudly that there's a terrible whiff in the air and really kick up a fuss about it; dead mice, clogged drains, and unappetizing lunches are all popular diversionary sources of pong. Keep up your campaign of scent sleuthing, sniffing all over the office like a drugs dog on the Thailand to Ibiza flight, until you reach the zenith of your stinky colleague, scurry round their workspace looking for potential sources until they finally take the hint.

P.S.: The over-perfumed deserve a note here, too. From the heavy, sweet, sensory-torturing scents (think the one that shares a name with a Robbie Williams song oft played at funerals) that send a migraine-shaped message to your poor suffocating brain, to the over-cologned guy who wears exactly the same scent as your recent ex-boyfriend and thus makes you want to weep every time you walk past him on the way to the photocopier, too much can almost be as bad as not enough.

GIVE A GIFT

This can be as thinly or thickly veiled as your moral compass allows you to be. Try one of the following:

The Stinker

• "They were giving out free samples of soap/deodorant/industrial cleaner at my station, I grabbed a handful, anyone want one?"

• "I know you mentioned you liked my perfume/aftershave the other day, it's actually this deodorizing body spray and I had a spare at home so I've bought you one in." (Whether or not they did comment on your perfume is entirely superfluous, just brazen it out with an "Oh it wasn't you, well have it anyway... no really, have it").

• "It's my friend's birthday tonight but they've suddenly died/slept with my boyfriend/remembered they got their date of birth wrong so now I'm left with this huge gift basket of deodorizing products that she specifically asked for. Would YOU like them instead?"

• Forego all words and simply leave a large can of deodorant on their desk. A problem perspiration variety if you really need to hit home.

BLAME YOURSELF

You'll need to get quite close for this one, so take a deep breath and scooch up as near as your one lungful of clean air will allow. Then exclaim loudly about what a terrible smell there is and how you must have forgotten your deo that morning. Really overdo your protestations until you drive a wedge of doubt into the true offender's mind about the true locale of the offending odor.

Not just one for the girls, a Bitch is a Bitch regardless of which bathroom they use. (Of course, you probably all have fashionable unisex bathrooms à la *Ally McBeal* now but you see what we're getting at.) Read on for the most common types of he- and she-bitches.

THE QUEEN BEE

Probably the prettiest, loudest, most attention-seeking person in the office with a gang of acolytes hanging off their every word, they've lived their whole life as if it were one long prom and they were vying to be king or queen. If you get on their wrong side you'll feel the icy force of their protective gang.

DEAL WITH IT: Channel Lindsay Lohan. No, don't start foregoing underwear and considering rehab as your holiday home, instead hit the QB Bitch where it hurts. The scales. Your QBB is probably wise to *Mean Girls'* Regina George's downfall at the hands of calorie-laden Kalteen bars, so you'll have to get a little more sneaky. Cream instead of almond milk in their lattes is a good place to start and a few spoonfuls of sugar in each and every green juice they've left in the fridge will soon start to add up. It won't stop them being mean to you, but it'll give you heaps of satisfaction.

THE IN THE BOSS'S POCKET

This little madam (or indeed mister) lives to brown nose. Painfully aware that they're never going to get anywhere with hard work and talent (being capable of neither), they've made the decision that the only way to get on at work is to become almost completely lodged in the lower intestine of the boss. They'll be keeping a dossier on the five minutes you're late every day, poking holes in each project you work on, and keeping all the emails you ever send, combing them nightly for anything they could possibly send on to your superiors.

DEAL WITH IT: VERY carefully. The ITBP Bitch is never off duty so it may be necessary to borrow war tactics and invent an intricate code as the only means of communicating when they're around.

The Bitch

THE JELLYFISH

"That's a lovely dress, Sarah. I had one a bit like that a few years ago, before I lost weight. Oh Steve, bless you for making a big effort and trying to use Powerpoint when you obviously don't have a clue, hope you didn't waste too much time on it?" Sound familiar? Then you've already identified your Jellyfish Bitch. Too wimpy to out and out insult you, they bury their barbs so the sting of their rudeness often only hits you as you walk away.

DEAL WITH IT: Play dumb. When you come across one of their landmines, don't give in to the explosion, instead admire the lovely topsoil covering it, play up the positive element of their insult and make it long-winded and boring to boot. "This dress, you really like it? Well thank you so much, let me tell you a story about it. I was shopping with my mum, or was it my sister, and we both saw it and at first we weren't sure, you know how sometimes you can't make up your mind…" zzzzzzzzzz. They won't be wasting their time with you again.

THE INTIMIDATOR

She once saw half of *The Devil Wears Prada* and has now confused running a regional branch of a medical equipment supplier with being the editor-in-chief of the world's biggest magazine. Shouting and screaming is her stock-in-trade, believing she's creating the perfect climate of fear in which to get maximum productivity from her employees. Trembling and tears are her favorite things to see in meetings and rumor has it she has specially lowered chairs in her office so when you're getting a bollocking she can tower over you at all times.

DEAL WITH IT: Affect sudden onset deafness. Remain completely oblivious to her raised voice until she's screeched herself hoarse and has exhausted her decibel level. Then say: "Oh sorry, were you talking to me, it's just I've had this nasty ear infection and lost 90% of my hearing. Can you put it in an email?"

THE WANTS YOUR JOB

AKA Baby Bitch, this person, usually fairly junior in the company, doesn't see why the fact you're still alive and kicking and in employment should be any barrier to them having your job. They'll stop at nothing to try and make you look incompetent and are praying for the day you get sacked/pregnant/dismembered.

DEAL WITH IT: Trick them—dealt with properly the WYJ Bitch is an incredibly useful asset as you can fool them into doing huge amounts of your work for you. Gussy up fobbing your tasks off on them as "developmental goals" and "personal progression," then sit back and let them get on with it.

THE OUT AND OUT

This person is just plain mean. Who knows why. Maybe they weren't hugged enough as a child. Maybe they haven't got laid this millennium. Completely lacking in empathy or kindness, they don't give an F if you or anyone else doesn't like them.

DEAL WITH IT: If you're of the impression a mass *Murder on the Orient Express*-inspired slaying with a letter opener might be a little OTT, then what about killing them with kindness? Maybe, just maybe, you'll be able to melt that stony heart?

In a post-David-Brent universe, you'd think these blights on the workplace might have receded a bit due to their very existence being dissected and vilified the world over. But no, they're still displaying their "you don't have to be mad to work here but it helps" signs with pride and donning novelty ties every holiday and high day they can. With a list of annoying habits that could fill an entire book, we've highlighted the ones truly worth serving time in prison for (post you assaulting them with a hole punch).

THE WITTY AUTO REPLY

Unable to turn off the wacky factor, even when they're not physically there to torture you with it, The Comedian's version of haunting you from the grave is the hilarious auto reply. Popular choices include:

• "I'm out of the office right now. Probably at a job interview! If I don't get it, I'll get back to you!!!" We pray you get it.

• "I'm currently laying on a tropical beach topping up my tan #donthateme." Already do mate, already do.

• "I'm out of the office and have limited access to emails (and my wife will kill me if I turn the iPhone on one more time!)" Like you have a wife.

THE INSANE EXCITEMENT ON ANY KIND OF CHARITY DAY

Comic Relief/Red Cross/Kittens Against ISIS, whatever the charity nothing gets a Comedian's sap rising like the chance to play the giddy goat all under the guise of a good cause. Maybe they'll ask you to sponsor them to do something wacky (they never quite got over the death of the baked bean bath as fundraiser), probably they'll wear something quirky all day—underpants over suit trousers/afro wig/Elton John glasses—and they'll definitely invite you to a special "gig" they're doing, all to raise a little extra (extra profile for them that is).

THE PRANK

The modern office offers many chances to get one over on your co-workers, all in the name of banter. From changing the Facebook status of anyone foolish enough to remain logged in (it's always a toilet or coming-out-related "Frape") to altering a screensaver to something mildly pornographic, the computer desktop is The Comedian's number one place to start.

If you're dealing with an older example, though, they might go a little more "IRL" in their jokes. Sellotaping a picture of themselves to the back of the toilet seat with a speech bubble saying "I'm watching you" is an oft-reported case of hilarity, as is any misappropriation of regular office supplies. A desk completely covered in Post-its or your chair wrapped in bubble wrap both scream "I'm a funny guy."

Finally, there's the "putting in the hours" kind of prank; one that's irresistible to the veteran joker. Whether it's scattering cress seeds in your keyboard (we think that's actually damaging company property, wiseass) or the classic "putting essential equipment into jelly," an hour spent pissing your colleagues off is an hour well spent in The Comedian's book.

The Comedian

Like the weekly fire alarm test, The Drama Queen provides the office with a regular, annoying, impossible-to-ignore, high-pitched siren as she sobs into her phone over her latest break-up/weight gain/fish bereavement/canceled SoulCycle class. She's still in recovery over the office downgrading to two-ply Kleenex and considers tears as much a part of her daily routine as her hourly calls to her mother.

Don't underestimate her, though, the weapons of a drama monarch are surprisingly effective. While they're throwing a toddler-esque strop and shaming Gwyneth Paltrow with their crocodile tears, what's the first thing you do? Well, unless you're the office Sociopath (more on them later), chances are you'll say something like: "Oh don't worry about that report/email/fact you've stolen my lunch for the third time running, it's really not a big deal" and let them get away with it! Add to this the fact that when she runs out of her own drama (it takes a while but occasionally there's a fallow period) she looks around for the merest hint of any gossip that she can spin into something to keep her entertained. Be careful, you could find yourself at the center of one of her latest palavers.

**The Drama
Queen Or King**

HOW TO DEAL WITH IT:

FIND A PARENT Hunt around for anyone who's a parent to a two-year-old—they'll know how to handle a brat.

REMOVE THE AUDIENCE A diva is nothing without an audience so, as they kick off about their latest crisis, just get up and walk away. If they question you just mumble something about diarrhea, even the most advanced DQ can't argue with that.

ASK IF THEY HAVE AN ALLERGY
As they sit and sob—and asking them what's wrong becomes impossible not to do—why not try handing them an antihistamine and pretending you thought their red puffy eyes and double rivers of snot were due to a reaction to a new product the cleaners must be using? (Note: Expect them to be absent from work the next day due to this idea you've given them.)

ARE YOU ONE?

YOU NEVER HAVE A COLD; IT'S ALWAYS THE FLU You attach yourself to every drama going, even if it affects you in no way. "What do you mean they're changing the brand of urinal cake in the gents?" says the person minus the equipment with which one would use aforementioned urinal.

YOU LOVE A CONSPIRACY THEORY "The reason Dan just slammed that meeting room door isn't because the hinge is dodgy, it's because he was seen coming out of Mike's office last week in a foul mood and ever since then Mike's been taking on more of the orders and Anna, who works with Mike, has told you that... ohhh is anyone even still awake?"

YOU KEEP KLEENEX IN YOUR DRAWER FOR TEARS NOT COLDS A molehill is always a mountain. A minor inconvenience of an out-of-order elevator results in several complaints and one full meltdown as you can't take the stairs due to an allergy/Achilles problem/chance of bumping into ex-office romance in the stairwell.

He probably has had a previous job selling houses (which he'll describe as something like chief residential negotiator) and he's definitely watched *The Wolf of Wall Street* (twice). He's also got the book, too, but he hasn't read it: "Fiction is for mugs and old ladies." The only books he reads (on his two weeks in Vegas) are entrepreneurs' autobiographies. He "done" Branson's last year and has Jobs' ready on his Formica display unit waiting to be packed for June's jaunt.

He's picked up a fair few insider tips from his hardbacks ("They just look better, don't they? Wouldn't catch Donald Trump walking round with no girly paperback") and attempts to bring a little of the New York stock exchange or Trump Towers boardroom to his third-floor corner cubicle. Sadly the effect is somewhat dampened when his "buy, buy, buy, sell, sell, sell" chatter refers to the industrial cleaning product he's now account manager of.

Spending around four-fifths of his wage on his monthly car payments, he'll make the journey in (from his mother's house) every day in his limited edition Subaru, despite the fact a train would take a quarter of the time, and he then has to spend the remaining fifth on a car park. As an added bonus the journey in his beloved baby allows him to keep up with his hair-gazing routine. He needs to check at least once every 20 minutes that it's perfectly placed to minimize his receding hairline. Anyway, he'll have a space in the executive car park in a year or two, once this latest deal comes off and he's supplying around 30% of his cleaning catchment area. Then he'll have his name in asphalt alright.

Capable of assaulting all of your senses, bar taste, in less than a minute (and if you're getting close enough to lick him, then you deserve everything you get). He's identifiable 20 seconds before he walks into a room by his signature scent—a mixture of mid-range aftershave, Little Trees "new car scent" air freshener, and what he thinks is testosterone but you'll identify as "jacket in need of a dry clean." On to the visuals and you could be forgiven for thinking he'd just come from performing a magic show for a group of toddlers but, no, he just thinks a waistcoat makes him look powerful (and slimmer). Next, your ears are in for a bashing once he starts churning out his business mantras; on a regular day he'll have clocked up five "work hard, play hards" and a handful of variations along the lines of "I could sell ice to the Eskimos" by lunchtime.

The Wide-boy Salesman

Ok, that guy in design might wear the nerdy glasses, don the fleece, and walk the walk—in orthopedic-style footwear—but in reality he's probably just a hipster jumping on the normcore bandwagon. And the girl on reception with kooky hair and prescription specs? She just thinks she's Zooey Deschanel. With true geekdom getting harder and harder to spot you might not even know if you're one yourself. So how can you identify the resident nerd?

GEEK SPOTTING

Answer yes to half of these and chances are you're the office Geek:

• Is "Have you turned it off and on again?" one of your most oft-repeated sentences at work?

• Have you ever played Dungeons and Dragons?

• Have you ever read a comic as an adult?

• Do you know where on your TV stations to find the SyFy channel?

• Is being able to complete a Rubik's Cube in under a minute something you'd list on your CV?

• Do you leave for work at precisely the same time, down to the second, every day?

• Do you know what LARP stands for?

• Have you ever taken part in LARP?

• Do you have any figurines on your desk? (Ok calm down, we didn't call them dolls.)

• Would you have an argument with a colleague over which Harry Potter school house you think they'd be in?

• Do you know more than the first three digits of Pi?

• Have you ever read fan fiction online?

• Have you ever written fan fiction?

• Have you ever got into an online argument about fan fiction?

• Ever taken a day off work to queue up to buy a computer game?

• Do you own more than one edition of *Star Wars*?

• Are you offended by *The Big Bang Theory*? (the show, not the scientific explanation).

The Geek

THE SOCIOPATH AKA THE ONE

Statistics say 4% of the world is made up of sociopaths. Now that doesn't really sound like much does it? You probably wouldn't bet on a football team that only had a 4% chance of winning and you consider today's lunch that only had 4% fat as a pretty big tick for your diet, but break it down. What 4% means in reality is that one in 25 of your colleagues probably secretly wants to murder you. Are you sitting next to one?

TYPES OF PSYCHO

If you come across any of these characters, quit your job immediately:

1. ANIMAL HATER Do they respond in a negative way to your daily LOLcat emails? Refused to take part in the pinboard of office pets? Didn't even flinch when Becky bought her house rabbit in for an office tour? Animal hatred is a surefire sign.

2. WHERE ARE THEY? They work strange hours, sometimes seemingly never going home and at other times disappearing with no reason for hours or days at a time. Their boss doesn't say anything because they're too terrified.

3. RIGHT AND WRONG? WHO GIVES ONE? They have no conscience whatsoever. This ranges from the trivial—thinking nothing of taking the chocolate on the desk you've been saving all day or using the last form in the pile without photocopying another so that everyone has to desperately search around for the master copy—to the major: dripping Tipp-Ex in your coffee or secreting toxins in the air vent when they've had enough of you.

**The Sociopath
AKA The One
You Think Might
Be A Murderer**

4. EMPATHY? WHAT'S THAT? Your whole family may very well have got wiped out in a freak hurricane/sandstorm/avalanche of cheese this weekend but to The Sociopath this registers no more than the change of biro suppliers. It's likely you could have a full-blown coronary while sitting at the next desk and they wouldn't even turn their head.

5. LEAVE ME ALONE They'll read their newspaper on breaks, lunch alone, avoid social occasions as if half the workforce had recently overcome Ebola, and have never knowingly made eye contact with anyone else in the office.

6. NEAT FREAK Is everything on their desk lined up at perfect 90-degree angles? Have you never seen so much as a stray staple infiltrate their neatness? All the better for avoiding forensic evidence and fingerprints, my dear.

CHAPTER 2
THE RULES OF...

There have been wars launched with less strategy than that which it takes to truly win in the sphere of office coffee or tea making. With an ideal ratio of cups made to cups drunk looking something like the male to female split on a Leonardo DiCaprio yacht holiday, spending a little time and effort learning how to effectively shirk your drink-making duties is vital. Below are some valuable tactical ploys to add to your arsenal:

THE LAST-MINUTE CALL

Not one for the faint-hearted or the very thirsty, this is effectively playing chicken with the person offering to make hot drinks. When they make their initial suggestion that they might be off to the kitchen to put the kettle on, make sure you get the fact you definitely don't want a cup in early and loudly. Let everyone else say yes. Allow time for one or two people to offer to help carry/pour/open doors but still hold back from confirming that you do indeed wish to be part of this coffee run. Wait another minute or two, then hit them with it, just as they're far enough away to be en route to the kitchen, but still near enough to hear: "Oh, do you know what, as you're going I will have one after all." This subtle delaying of joining in somehow negates you from officially taking part in this round and thus avoids you owing your colleagues the next time.

P.S.: Don't try this on elderly colleagues—not because it's unfair as they might find walking/carrying/standing up more difficult than others, but because they might be deaf and miss your last-minute shout.

Coffee Rounds

THE RENEGADE

Of course, the easiest way to avoid rounds is not to drink regular coffee or tea at all, but this doesn't mean you have to miss out on all the laziness of getting everyone else to make your beverages for you. Simply pick something that isn't coffee—from lemon and hot water or jasmine tea to hot chocolate, you are outside the remit. Choices are plenty and can always be tacked onto the coffee round without responsibilities. After all, you don't even drink coffee.

THE BRIBER

This is one to fall back on when you've pretty much exhausted all other options and your colleagues are adopting Cold War tactics in freezing you out of any coffee rounds. Bring in a supply of posh cookies or a fancy cake, let everyone catch a glimpse of this delicious treat but get it in their minds early that its only to come out when it can be enjoyed properly—with a perfectly made hot drink. Don't give in at the first cup, though; you've spent cash on this and managed properly it should give you at minimum a day's drink-making respite as return on your investment.

THE PROCRAS-TEA-NATOR

Another example of tactical power play, this time you make plenty of noise about the fact you are DEFINTELY about to go and make tea or coffee. Get the thought of a delicious cup in everyone's mind, maybe even stand up as if heading off on this thirst-sating mission, then you suddenly remember you've got something really important to do and immediately become absorbed in furiously typing an urgent email, or pick up the phone where you're inconceivably put on hold for 10 minutes. Keep up the pretense of caffeine cravings throughout these diversionary moves, adding to your colleagues desire until finally a weaker member snaps and offers to go themselves.

Coffee Rounds

THE PURPOSEFULLY TERRIBLE

A handy one to pull out in a new workplace—make it known nice and early that you're totally and utterly hopeless at creating hot drinks. Volunteer eagerly and frequently for coffee rounds, but from your very first attempt get as much wrong as you can conceivably get away with. Be it poor temperature control—who has time to wait for the kettle to boil? Over- or under-sugaring are also easy "mistakes" to make, and for the pro try making it so weak that it's barely beige on the Pantone scale, or so strong that it'd almost qualify as a solid. Colleagues whose laziness is more pronounced than their taste buds at first may be immune to this trick, so you might have to move onto the sublevel of poor drink-making—the gross out. This entails finding the grubbiest, murkiest looking cups in which to make tea or coffee. You might have to improvise with the odd lipstick smear or food dribble round the edge of one or two to really send the message home that you cannot be trusted in the kitchen.

Nothing cements your social standing in the office like a birthday. Just like when no one from your class came to your seventh birthday party 'cos it was cake and ice cream, not burgers and Laser Quest, an unacknowledged office birthday is a huge **EVERYBODY HATES YOU** smack in the face. That accepted, the over-acknowledged office b'day with its enforced sense of organized fun is just plain awkward for everyone. Oh FFS why were you even born in the first place, then you wouldn't have this problem...

Office Birthdays

CAKE

Everyone likes cake right? WRONG. No one likes cake anymore. They like marshmallows with their Instagram selfies printed on them or artisan Pantone-color-of-the-year-shaded meringues. Cupcakes are deader in the water than the Costa Concordia and despite a valiant effort the unfortunate cake pop failed to win over any hearts and minds. But despite this universal back turning, there's still one day a year where you've got to have cake. Actually it's not even one day a year 'cos you've also got to awkwardly pretend to enjoy a bit of dry old Victoria sponge for everyone else's bloody birthday, too. It'd be ok if it was good cake but, of course, it never is 'cos the buyer—be it the b'dayer themselves or whichever poor soul in the office is in charge of such things—will be spending the least cash to get the most cake and they probably don't like any of you anyway, so what do they care if you have to force down what's essentially sweetened sawdust.

Hastily hacked into using the wrong end of a spoon because no one can find a knife, you'll pay cake roulette as to whether you have to endure a huge chunk or luck out with a tiny slither. Then you'll have to eat it over a makeshift plate of a torn-up bit of paper towel while hovering awkwardly round the photocopier making hideous small talk. If you're very lucky someone with a hitherto unknown nut allergy might suddenly collapse to the floor with a severe allergic reaction because the cake was bought in the same place as someone who once ate a peanut once walked past, thus bringing the whole unbearable tradition to a swift end.

WHIP ROUND

Everyone knows the rules for the office whip round. Much as the debate of if a tree falls in the forest but no one sees it, did it really happen yada yada, if there's no one around when the whip round envelope comes to your desk and you don't really like the person, then you're definitely not putting anything in. Conversely, if it's someone you really hate, not just a colleague you feel a mild level of ennui about, then putting in a laughable amount is actually more satisfying than giving nothing, and rids you of loose change into the bargain. Keep a small pot of coppers on your desk for such occasions and you'll be surprised at the level of satisfaction you feel when they email round thanking the office for their book token knowing that your couple of coppers helped in no way.

BIRTHDAY DRINKS

Now this is the worst bit for the birthday boy/girl. In reality, you may hate every single person you work with but if you're unlucky enough for your birthday to fall on a Thursday or Friday, you just know the crowd is going to be baying for birthday drinks. At best this might only have to consist of a number of bad bottles of wine placed around the now decimated remains of your earlier substandard birthday cake and you'll get away with half a warm glass of acidic wine before pretending you've got to dash off for terribly intricate birthday plans. At worst you're going to have to spend all night with these people. Even if you don't mind half of them, office etiquette means you'll have to send a department-wide email, thus opening it up to each and every person that not only makes your nine-to-five hell but also now has the power to ruin your birthday.

TO SING OR NOT TO SING

Here's a clue: it's the latter. This isn't pre-school and apart from Dave in facilities who once queued for 14 hours to audition for *X Factor*, and Amy in accounts who lists karaoke competitions as one of her hobbies, no one enjoys the sound of their own voice and will stare at their feet for the whole embarrassing 90 seconds that the awkward rendition of Happy Birthday takes. The poor recipient has no choice but to adopt a terrible frozen half smile reminiscent of those stroke commercials and try to focus on not passing out through embarrassment.

Office Birthdays

THE COMMUNAL CARD

Oh god, the pressure to write something witty and/or meaningful and/or sucky uppy if it's your boss; the realization that everyone who hasn't already signed it is going to see what you've written and think you're an asshole, a suck up, or an uncaring, unfunny bastard; and the fact that this all needs to be done as the office administrator hangs over you waiting for you to finish means that more office heart attacks take place* during the writing of communal greetings cards than while performing any other activity in the workplace.

* probably

It can both be the highlight of your working day, and the worst hour of your nine-to-five. Negotiating a successful lunch is no mean feat, everyone knows the crushing disappointment of a dissatisfying midday meal and remembers the spirit-raising potential of a lunch break well spent. Here are the pitfalls to watch out for to ensure you fall in the latter camp:

PROBLEM A: THE OFFICE FRIDGE

If someone suggested you kept your underpants in the same drawer as everyone else you worked with, chances are you'd suddenly see the benefits of going commando, but whereas we'd all balk at the thought of our gussets sharing space with those of our colleagues, we're more than happy to take our chances with what goes in our mouths. Welcome to the office fridge. It's a scary place.

1. THEFT The most common fridge-based crime is, without exception, theft. Whether it's the sneaky pilfering of an almost unnoticeable amount of your lunch—think half a handful of grapes or an all but negligible amount of carrot batons—or a full-blown misappropriation of both rounds of your carefully prepared sandwiches, workplace fridge raiders can, and will, ruin your day. Conducting their thievery with precision and stealth, witnesses of the culprit are rare and positive identification even rarer.

DEAL WITH IT: If you're suffering a run of lunchtime larceny, then bring out the big guns and hit the thief with a nasty surprise. Replace your usual sandwich filling with something disgusting; maybe tuna for cat food. You might not find out who the thief is (unless you sit right opposite the bathrooms) but chances are they won't do it again.

2. REFUSING TO OWN UP TO GONE OFF FOOD

We've all done it. In a fit of economy, decided to give up our daily sushi habit and bring in sandwiches from home (that actually ended up costing three times as much once we factored in the price of artisan bread/acquisition of three new condiments/amount of food we ended up throwing out when we gave up on it after one day), only for lunch to come around and us be swayed by the fact it's Dave's birthday/two-for-one at the pub/what looked tasty last night now looks as appealing as a sober kebab and we've said, "Screw it, I'll eat my homemade lunch tomorrow and treat myself today." The problem is you feel exactly the same the day after. And the day after that… And before you know it your Tupperware container harbors germs the World Health Organization would issue a warning about. As the weeks pass you think you'll sneak it out when no one's watching but the chance never comes (just how does the fridge thief do it?) and, as it joins the unofficial mausoleum of other decaying food containers, it soon becomes entirely untouchable.

DEAL WITH IT: Stop lying to yourself that you can kick the daily lunch-buying habit. Ain't ever gonna happen.

3. ABUSE OF COMMUNAL MILK

Frankly it's a miracle that your company is still providing this daily ration of dairy, maybe they realize that keeping you in the office for your hot drink fix gives them at least another 15 minutes hard labor a day that otherwise you might fritter away in Starbucks. However, even those companies that adopt an extremely liberal attitude to milk allocation will not be able to keep up with the demands of the communal milk abuser. Disregarding the unwritten rule that it's for hot drinks only, the abuser plays fast and loose with your rations, drinking entire cups of the stuff cold, creating no-water hot chocolate, and, worst of all, chucking it on their morning cereal, leaving you with a mere splash for your first coffee of the day. Ugh.

DEAL WITH IT: This takes a little bit of prep, but a few days before you plan to really teach them a lesson, remove a carton from the fridge and keep it somewhere warm, maybe kill two birds with one stone and hide it against the overheating computer tower of your least-favored colleague. Check frequently on the progress of its degradation; too lumpy and the abuser will be forewarned, not gone-off enough and it might not register on their milk-loving taste buds. Then, just when it's at the optimum ratio of undetectable/disgusting, follow them into the kitchen with it concealed upon your person, distract them before they reach for the fridge (try telling them something's going for free in the corridor—if they're this grabby with milk they're bound to be a right glutton for anything gratis), and then do the old switcheroo with the one you prepared earlier. Should put them off their greedy guzzling ways for a few weeks at least.

ONE MORE THING

As an addendum to fridgiquette, and while we're on the subject of white goods, we have to mention the microwave. If you do any of the following when using this, chances are everyone hates you:

1. Take other people's food out before it's done.

2. Try to skip the line 'cos you're only "popping something in for 30 seconds." Newsflash: That's what everyone else is doing, love, it ain't a slow cooker.

3. Fail to grasp how a microwave works. Hint: Metal sets on fire and if you don't prick it before you press start, then you're going to cause an explosion.

4. Not clearing up aforementioned lack-of-pricking explosions.

5. Air pollution. For the love of god think about how last night's salmon is going to affect those around you.

PROBLEM B: SMELLS

You know the saying "one man's poison is another man's meat"? Well that could have been written about your lunch. You might be anticipating some delicious delicacy, but remember there's probably going to be at least one person whose stomach you're going to send into gymnastics. With that in mind it's obvious you can't please all of the people all of the time, but here's what to avoid to piss off the least amount of colleagues:

FISH A no-brainer. Cold is just about acceptable if you eat it quickly, but add any form of heat to the equation and you're asking for trouble. When was the last time you heard anyone say, "Oh wow that heated-up fish really smells great!" N.B. Sushi—because of its cool factor and the fact that half the time the nearest it has got to fish is the boat the veggies wrapped in your rice were imported into the country on—does not count.

EGGS Long story short: they smell like sewers. If your colleagues wanted to go into the sanitation industry they would have done. And they'd probably be getting paid more into the bargain.

BROCCOLI/CABBAGE Hark back to the smelly kid at school. That's you and your wilting greens in the microwave, that is.

MEAT A wide category, but when it comes to heating up meaty dishes there's a fine line between home-cooked yumminess and "Is that your lunch or someone's pungent BO?" Beef tends to give off a particularly armpit-esque smell, especially if there are onions or garlic in the mix. Anything curried will mark you out as a lunch leper.

Conversely, if you're polishing off something that smells delicious, you'll probably equally infuriate your colleagues if you don't offer to share. Can't win, can you? Best to just eat freeze-dried dehydrated foodstuffs like spacemen in the 1980s.

Lunch Politics

THE WORST OF THE REST

By no means an exhaustive list of office-based eating issues, here are those that can't go minus a mention:

THE CONSTANT GRAZER Like the worst person to sit next to in the cinema, the constant grazer spends the whole day chewing away in some kind of tranquilized bovine daze. Shoveling their snack of choice into their mouth with all the regularity of an automated forklift, there won't be a second of your day when your ears aren't full of their rustling, masticating, and salivating.

THE FEEDER Probably the person with the best body in the office, the feeder loves nothing more than encouraging others to break their diets. Armed with all kinds of tempting treats and a cookie jar that never, ever falls empty, for every calorie you eat they see it as two they don't.

THE COOKIE TRUFFLER Were your cookie-scoffing colleague born a pig they would have been worth their weight in gold, such is their ability to snuffle out treats. Sensing the opening of a packet with the dexterity of Sherlock Holmes during a particularly tricky Sudoku puzzle, they must surely burn off half of the fat they're about to consume with their lightening-fast sprint to your desk. N.B. The biscuit truffler would never knowingly purchase their own biscuits. That would defeat the object.

Remember back when we first got email how exciting getting a new one was? Hearing that *Sleepless in Seattle* "You've got mail!" ping was the highlight of our day, actually screw highlight of the day, we only got one (usually from our cousin in Australia) every three weeks, so those three lines and low-res photo pretty much made our year. Now you've definitely switched off any kind of aural notification because if you had to listen to that ping 17 times a minute every hour of your working day, you'd definitely have thrown your computer/self out of the nearest window (well you'd try, but of course you don't actually have any windows that open due to your company's air policy) and a new email is as welcome as scabies.

THE KISS x

Now this is very industry dependent. If you work in anything vaguely media-y or French, then the kiss at the end of your mail is practically compulsory. In fact, if you limit it to just one you'll probably be considered rude and standoffish.

Three is probably a crowd, though, so stick to a pair. Anything outside of these affection-friendly industries and you're in somewhat of a kiss minefield. Send a kiss to the strange guy who sits in the corner when you don't really know what he does and it could look like an invitation for a sexual liaison on the staircase. It's not all negative, though, the kiss is a handy way of giving someone a passive-aggressive bollocking. Sign off with two at the end of a right telling off and you'll still look like the good guy.

COMPANY ALL

There's a special place in hell for people who abuse company all. From the person who can't work out the difference between reply and reply all, to the dicks in publicity who use it to let the rest of the workforce in on the "hilarious" in-jokes that only three or four people actually get via the guy who thinks it's his own personal eBay—"Lovely Ikea rose print for sale as I'm off traveling, collection only"—and the 34 people who feel it necessary to reply all to a company all saying please take me off this chain, each and every one of you is contributing to make your colleagues day just that bit worse. Happy with yourself?

YOUR SIGN OFF

Firstly, you don't really need one. This isn't a class in school on how to correctly write a formal letter. Do you lay your address out in the top right corner when composing an email? No, you don't, so you can ditch all of the following:

YOURS FAITHFULLY Calm down, it's an email not a 19th-century plight of troth.

KIND REGARDS What if it's not a kind email? What if it's writing to an employee telling them they're being sacked for sexual harassment. That's not very kind is it?

BEST WISHES Are you writing this from a senior citizens' care home?

LOOKING FORWARD TO HEARING FROM YOU Reply now or I'll end you.

TALK SOON I'll call you about this every hour, on the hour, until you reply.

TAKE CARE This is the last contact I wish to have with you. Ever.

CHEERS MATE I wear novelty socks to work.

THX I draw my i's with a heart instead of a dot!

DO'S AND DON'TS

DO: Think, "Could I google this?" Could you get the answer to this email in three seconds by using Google? Will the reader get you that answer by using Google? Well bloody google it then.

DO: Be aware that using the urgent/high priority button makes you look like a dick. No one looks at these on emails anyway. They'll read it when they read it.

DO: Remember that oddly shaped thing on your desk that occasionally makes a funny noise. THE PHONE. You're not a 13-year-old evolved only to type (at least we hope you're not and if you're 13 and already in an office you've got more pressing issues like child labor to be thinking about), so would a quick phone call save an email chain that'll go on for days?

DON'T: Fake like you're already in a conversation with the person by putting a sneaky RE: in the subject head.

DON'T: Bitch or attempt to conduct an office romance on work email. That's what WhatsApp is for.

DON'T: Put an annoying quote in your email signature, yes it was cute when you saw it typed over the top of a latte on Instagram but nobody needs to read about today being a gift and that's why we call it the present every bloody time you send them an email about late invoices.

DON'T: Use read receipt requests. No one in the history of the workplace has ever typed yes to send one of these. Stop spying on us; you'll know we've read it when you get a reply.

DON'T: Do a follow-up phone call two minutes after sending the email. "I just sent you an email, did you get it?" NO BECAUSE I AM NOT A CYBORG THAT CAN PROCESS 1,000 WRITTEN WORDS A MINUTE.

DON'T: Get your BCC and CC mixed up. If you get confused just remember the B stands for bitch, as in you're being one by not letting on to the original recipient just who can see this.

With the advent of hot desking we could be losing a valuable tool to determine how much of a tool those who sit around us are. From the obligatory kid's graduation picture sitting astride the windowsill to the inspirational quote carved onto a porcelain heart hanging from the side of a computer, the personal ephemera your co-workers choose to decorate/desecrate their workspace with gives vital clues to their personality type.

FLOWERS—SELF-PURCHASED

WHAT IT TELLS YOU: They've got to the "you need to love yourself before anyone else can love you" chapter in their latest self-help book.

EXOTIC BEACH PHOTO

WHAT IT TELLS YOU: I probably earn more than you.

PHOTO COLLAGE OF A SASSY GALS' NIGHT OUT

WHAT IT TELLS YOU: Do not ask me if I have a boyfriend, I'm fine single thank you. Yes. Really.

FLOWERS—SENT IN

WHAT IT TELLS YOU: Their boyfriend is probably cheating on them. Or he's worried she's cheating on him and is spraying his scent to ward off the office lothario.

ANYTHING WITH AN INSPIRATIONAL QUOTE

WHAT IT TELLS YOU: Not the brightest. They'd buy a turd if it had something Audrey Hepburn once said stuck on it.

Personal Possessions

TEDDY/TROLL/ANY KIND OF ANIMAL- OR TOY-BASED MASCOT

WHAT IT TELLS YOU: Hasn't had sex this decade.

LARGE HEADSHOT OF SIGNIFICANT OTHER

WHAT IT TELLS YOU: Firstly, check it definitely is their SO and not:
a) the picture that came with the frame
b) someone they're stalking
If it's one of these two options you need to look at it in an entirely different way.

TROPHIES/THANK YOU CARDS/CERTIFICATES

WHAT IT TELLS YOU: They want everyone to know how wonderful they are. They probably never won anything at school and are still sore over it.

AN "EXECUTIVE" TOY

WHAT IT TELLS YOU: This person is unaware it's not 1988. Has anyone checked them for a head injury?

It's an unfortunate fact that at some point in the day you're going to have to indulge in some mindless crap chat with a whole spectrum of colleagues. It's going to be painful. It's going to be the same every freaking day. And there's not a thing you can do about it...

LOCATION, LOCATION, LOCATION

The geography of small talk is key to the level of annoyance. If it starts somewhere with easy escape options, it's just about bearable; if it takes place in confinement you're likely to want to Van Gogh yourself deaf.

Small Talk

KITCHEN Theoretically relatively easy to walk away from but not if you've been waiting for the microwave to come free for ages, then you're stuck in a vortex of lunch chat. Those 180 seconds being counted down on the microwave feel like they're in some way breaking the traditional theories of time as three minutes of hearing about Jane's Weight Watchers fish pie feels like an entire day of food-based filibustering.

WATER COOLER The easiest to escape from, use this venue tactically to suck up with small talk, head over right when your superiors are rehydrating for the perfect time frame of ass-kissing chat.

LIFT Arguably the worst place to be caught, here there's literally no escape and you could be stuck next to ANYONE—from the chatty mailroom boy to the terrifying CEO. You're at the mercy of whoever's legs are too lazy to carry them up three flights of stairs. Stuck between the thought of the safety of silence and staring down at your iPhone and not wanting to look like the rudest bastard on your floor, will you succumb to commenting on how you're sure these elevators get slower every day? Whichever option you go for you'll hate yourself all day.

BATHROOM LINE Nobody wants to spend more time than they absolutely have to in their office bathroom but should you try and pass the time with a quick chat or stare down at the floor trying not to pee yourself until a cubicle comes free? We say the latter, mainly for the ick factor. What if the person you've just been idly discussing Taylor Swift's new boyfriend with goes into the can, then comes out having created a far from pleasing environment for you to go into next? You may have to briefly continue the conversation while trying not to inhale any of their noxious fumes. Best just to keep yourself to yourself.

ACCEPTABLE TOPICS OF DISCUSSION

If you really have to chat, try one of these:

YOUR COMMUTE If you keep it as brief as possible or something genuinely interesting did happen such as an arrest (criminal or medical), then we'll listen.

TIME LIMIT: You may wring no more than five minutes per day from this.

YOUR CHILDREN If we know you well enough to know their names, or at least be able to make a ballpark guess and could estimate roughly what age they are (i.e. more kindergarten than college), then if we like you we'll indulge you. But only if we're in a good mood.

TIME LIMIT: Around three to four minutes per child. Less if we're hungover.

WEATHER TBH we know what the weather's like today. We have iPhones. And eyes. But we'll accept that this is the cure-all of small talk and as such we'll pretend not to want to punch you in the face.

TIME LIMIT: Seconds not minutes.

GENERIC WORK BITCHING We'll save the real bitching for somewhere where the walls don't have ears but a generic moan about non-specific things that aren't really anyone's fault like the long wait for the elevator or the photocopier breaking down again are a good way to get an essential dose of low-level negativity into the working day. And who doesn't benefit from that?

TIME LIMIT: Are we bored? We'll give you 10, then.

UNACCEPTABLE TOPICS OF CONVERSATION

Unless you want a suicide on your conscience, avoid these:

FRIENDS WHO WE DON'T KNOW We really don't care how much of a bitch Claire was this weekend, nor how Paul never gets a round of drinks in BECAUSE WE DON'T KNOW THESE PEOPLE. Do we run up to strangers in the street and ask for a potted life history? We do not. Although it would probably be more interesting than hearing about your moronic tribe of acquaintances every day.

HEALTH BELOW THE WAIST If you've had a wisdom tooth out we'll listen and maybe offer a painkiller. Got a chest infection? We'll pop out for a Tylenol or two. Broken rib? We won't make you carry stuff. Anything around the pelvic region? We don't want to know, thank you very much. Keep the size of your fibroids and the amount of nighttime pees to yourself please.

GIVING BIRTH As above, times one thousand.

LOVE LIFE Is there a more dreaded question than "How's your love life?" Once only the preserve of embarrassing aunts, the dating axis has now shifted so far it's perfectly acceptable for someone you've spoken to twice in your life to enquire after the frequency of your bedroom activity. We blame Tinder.

Small Talk

Short of erecting a Saniflo in your desk drawers or catheterizing yourself there's no way to avoid using the office bathrooms. Here's how to make it as painless as possible:

DO'S

DO: Cultivate a favorite cubicle. It'll make it feel more like home.

DO: Think about trying out the facilities on other floors. Especially for "lengthier" trips; it's a lot more relaxing on the bowels knowing you're not going to have to make eye contact with a close colleague on the other side of the door. Plus they might be loads nicer than yours.

DO: Develop an understanding of peak times. Ten minutes before the end of the day (insurance pee to avoid having to use any kind of public transport convenience), just before lunch (don't want to waste a break peeing on your own time), and mid-afternoon (having a little rest to ward off your afternoon slump) are all times to avoid unless you want to be stuck in a none-too-fragrant bathroom forever.

DO: Practice good urinal etiquette. Never stand next to anyone unless it's absolutely necessary. There's no way you'll be able to project an efficient stream next to your boss and the last thing you want hanging over your appraisal is "weird pee-er."

DO: Wash your hands. Didn't your mother teach you anything?

DON'TS

DON'T: Acknowledge the fact that you've somehow managed to synch your toilet trips up with a stranger in the office. Once you've both been in there at the same time for the third day running you might be tempted to make a comment, but just don't.

DON'T: Hog a cubicle to do your make-up. There's no more annoying sound (yes, there are grosser but none quite as irritating) to come from a long-time closed toilet door than the constant rustling of a make-up bag. Buy a compact and do your mascara at your desk.

DON'T: Use a cubicle as your own personal callbox. Maybe you're not familiar with the concept of soundproofing but you don't have to be a studio engineer to work out that the three-inch gap at the top and bottom of the door might just mean everything you say can be heard outside.

DON'T: EVER take reading matter with you. No one wants to handle meeting notes that have borne witness to your latest evacuation.

DON'T: Hammer on the door if you suspect someone's dawdling; you have no clue of what might be going on in there.

The Bathroom

CHAPTER 3
HOW TO...

There are as many good ways to throw a sickie as there are good reasons to do so, therefore it's important to consider both of these factors before embarking on an illicit day off. Each situation requires a slightly different approach for maximum success, so study our guide for all skiving eventualities.

1. THE SUNNY DAY

You've woken up to an absolute scorcher and the last thing you want to do is to travel in the human sauna that you know your chosen mode of public transport will be. The beach/pool/beer garden is calling, but if you don't spend all day in a burkha and factor 90 your boss is going to realize that you probably didn't get your healthy glow/mahogany tan/third-degree burns (depending on the ratio of sun cream applied to booze drunk in aforementioned beer garden) from your sick bed.

HOW TO: This calls for the non-sick sickie AKA the household emergency. Something hot/dusty/noisy/potentially life-threatening is going on in your home. As a result, you have no choice but to take refuge outside or lose your life to the tsunami emanating from your battered old washing machine/fall unconscious due to gases emerging from your dodgy boiler.

DON'T: Overplay it too much. A broken boiler will probably be fixed in a day, whereas the entire roof caving in on your head means you're going to have to keep up the pretense of repairs for weeks to come.

2. THE HANGOVER

This isn't so much a desire as a necessity. When lifting even your head from the pillow causes vertigo unprecedented at ground level and you've vomited hitherto undiscovered shades of stomach bile, there's no way you're going anywhere.

HOW TO: Work with what you've got. Chances are that cheap white wine and those five cigarettes (you forgot you haven't smoked since 1998), not to mention the three-hour vomathon that started at 6am, have all combined to give you the kind of raspy voice that simply can't be faked. You're not even lying. You ARE extremely ill.

DON'T: Forget social media. Did you post anything last night about the "Awesum karokay seshun" back at yours at 4am? How likely is it that photographs of you licking tequila from the belly button of someone you thought was hot, but in the cold light of day is very much not, will appear on Instagram at lunchtime, when your mates who didn't have to work today finally surface?

Throw A Sickie

If you're not organized enough to have blocked all workmates with privacy settings that even the White House would deem draconian (and frankly who the hell even knows how to do that?), then you're going to need to be hyper vigilant. You'd better take down those incriminating statuses and snaps quicker than an A-list bachelor's PR quashes gay rumors. It'd almost be less stressful to go to work.

3. THE WEEKDAY WEDDING

So all of your friends have put their own selfish needs first and landed you with an entire season of Friday weddings. "Oh it'll be wonderful, everyone will get to enjoy a lovely long weekend," they think, while you're a little more of the "I'll be buggered if I'm wasting a precious day off on you, you inconsiderate bastards, I'm only coming 'cos I hope it's a free bar/I might get to frottage your fit cousin I've been stalking on Facebook" school of thought.

HOW TO: This is a situation where putting in the prep is key. You need to make sure people think you're ill enough not to be contacted all day, because if she needs to ring you, June from accounts isn't going to believe that your doctor's surgery has a house band blasting out an ever so slightly out of time YMCA in the waiting room. And a conference call with the head of European sales in the bathroom may be a little tricky over a backdrop of vomiting bridesmaids and rutting groomsmen.

For a guaranteed day of left-aloneness, all roads lead to diarrhea. But with the shits being as hackneyed an excuse as Emergency Room attendees claiming they simply tripped and fell on the tomato sauce bottle/electric toothbrush/gerbil lodged in their anal cavity, you need to make it more convincing. Do this by making noises the day before about the slightly weird-tasting tuna baguette you had for lunch or the sushi restaurant you're heading to that evening that's an unbelievably bargainous tenner for all you can eat. If you've got the acting skills you could even squeeze in a few dashes to the bathroom late in the afternoon, making sure your boss notices you bustling past, clutching your stomach in a state of clear agitation.

DON'T: Walk into the office with a massive overnight bag, especially one with a top hat/cone of confetti/lover of the bride t-shirt sticking out.

4. THE SPORTING EVENT

So you and your bros want to skive off, drink beers, and watch the big game? Well please do and spare the rest of us—the awful banter between sports fans as they try to follow match progress in the office is more painful than stepping barefoot onto an upturned plug.

HOW TO: Stay away from other office sport bores. In the run-up to game day, if your boss catches you talking about the World-National-Super-Mega-Kicksport Trophy, then the jig is up. Locking yourself in the bathroom for your entire lunchbreak is the only way you can avoid potentially incriminating sport-related chats. Don't worry, your non-sport-worshipping colleagues will somehow manage without your company.

DON'T: Talk about sports. Sure you might find this harder than David Beckham trying to recite his three times table, but you have to try.

5. THE MULTI DAYER

The mini break you don't have enough days left for, the desire to get out of a particular project, a general feeling of seriously CBA, whatever your reason for attempting a multi-day sickie, there's a golden rule for prolonged skiving. GO GYNAE! (P.S.: Boys, don't feel left out—urological complaints work just as well.)

HOW TO: You're going to need to do a little bit of research here. It's not school, so mere period pain will not elicit a free pass. Leave your dignity at the door and concentrate on finding the most embarrassing words you can—try chucking in the odd prolapse, discharge, or anything ending in -oscopy for guaranteed no questions asked.

DON'T: Attempt to ring this in. Unless you're calling in sick at your job as a gynaecological consultant there's no way you're going to be able to pronounce your obscure complaint and your colpoperineorrafia (it's a real thing, google it) will be much easier to text.

It's said that in order to achieve mastery in your field you need to dedicate at least 10,000 hours of practice to your chosen discipline. That claim diametrically opposes the view of the office idler, who has mastered the art of doing sweet FA by putting in as little effort as possible. What follows are simple methods to shirk your work-related responsibilities and enjoy a relaxingly unproductive career.

CC LOTS OF PEOPLE IN

Do you know what CC actually means? No it's not carbon copy, it's actually create cover. Think of it this way: If you send an email that takes you five minutes to write to just one person, then they're the only one who knows that you've been doing anything other than watching YouTube videos of cats falling off window ledges. CC a couple of others in unnecessarily and you're upping the percentage of people under the impression that you're actually doing something with your day.

Another way CC wins for you is that you're distributing the blame should anything mess up. Get yourself a rep for unnecessary CC action and NO ONE will ever bother to read to the bottom. (This tactic works even better if you bury the genuine info at the end of a long email chain in manner of a politician releasing bad news on the same day Kate Middleton has a different blow dry.) Ok so the budget report was kind of your thing but you did CC Barbara and Tom in, so really they should have been aware of the problems, so you know, whose fault is it really?

**Get Away With
Doing Nothing
At All**

THE LENGTHY BATHROOM BREAK

There are three little words that'll help you waste at least one-eighth of your day sitting daydreaming in your office bathroom: Irritable Bowel Syndrome. IBS is as much of a catch-all as nude-colored tights, even doctors don't really know what it is so what hope does Sue in HR have? Simply mumble it in the direction of your boss to unlock the opportunity for at least three 20-minute slots of me time per day. Hint: Make sure you save one of your Netflix device logins for your phone; you could clear one of those box sets on your "to watch" list in a month.

CREATE MORE MEETINGS

Nothing gives the impression of busyness like being completely impossible to get hold of—unfortunately, that doesn't include being incommunicado because you're sleeping off four lunchtime wines, or have sneaked out for a haircut/Brazilian/eyebrow wax. (Hint: Don't do the last one unless you have a handy excuse about contact dermatitis up your sleeve to explain away why your upper forehead seems to have suddenly spent the last hour on a Caribbean beach minus SPF.) Instead, get as much time as possible away from your computer/phone/nosily breathing colleagues (a guaranteed exemption for murder if ever we heard one) by arranging as many meetings as possible. The more people invited, and the greater irrelevancy to your job role, the better. Then all you have to do is sit back and daydream for 40 minutes or so. Set them in a darkened room with plenty of on-screen presentations and you might even fit in a snooze. As a final plus you might even be able to sneak in some catering, and there's no greater highlight in an office day than a free sandwich platter.

PUT YOUR EARPHONES IN

Imagine how much easier your day would be if you didn't have to talk to anyone. If you could somehow cut out any verbal contact whatsoever with your annoying customers, clients, and colleagues. Sounds like the dream? Well it's within your reach. In fact, it's probably in your handbag or pocket right now... simply reach in and pull out... your earphones. Clamp them on and everyone will presume you're terribly busy listening to some important transcript. Upgrade to those over-the-head, noise-silencing ones and everyone will soon know it's not worth the embarrassment of repeatedly calling out your name as you obliviously ignore them.

VOLUNTEER FOR MORE

This might sound like an oxymoron, but the more projects you're part of, the more excuses you have not to do anything with your day. Spread yourself thinner than full-fat butter on Kate Bosworth's morning slice of toast and you'll soon discover that you really don't have to do very much at all.

Get Away With Doing Nothing At All

HAVE A JOB THAT NOBODY UNDERSTANDS

Remember the "transponder" episode of *Friends*, where no one knows what Chandler does for a living? Well if the digital age has done anything at all for us, it has given us the luxury of literally hundreds of job titles that 99% of the rest of the company do not have the foggiest about; land one and you're laughing. Tell everyone that the complicated bit of native digital initializing should take around six weeks to complete, dash it off in the morning, and then spend the next five weeks and four days reading about the misdemeanors of Z-listers on TMZ.

Dante's *Inferno* describes nine circles of hell, but there is in fact a tenth—an all-day meeting sat next to Stinky Carl in IT following a night of alcohol-fueled excess. Here's how to survive the repercussions of two bottles of wine and three Jägerbombs:

MAKE LIKE A TRAMP

Look to those who drink professionally for a hint and conceal your drink. And no, we're not suggesting you wrap your vodka bottle in a third-hand McDonald's paper bag. Instead, if you're trying to pretend the closest you got to alcohol last night was a particularly vigorous rub-down with hand sanitizer, then you don't want your morning after the night before choice of beverage to give you away. Nothing screams "I'm still over the limit" like a pre-9am, full-fat Coke or a slowly sipped energy drink, so the smart boozers decant. Invest in one of those opaque sports bottles and fool everyone into thinking it's a protein shake.

NEVER CROWDFUND

A company-all email asking for painkillers? You might as well dump a urine sample on the desk of your boss.

DON'T BE SQUEAMISH

You know that without a nap you're very unlikely to make the end of the day, but with companies being somewhat stingy when it comes to providing day beds for the terminally hungover you're going to have to get creative. Put yourself in the mindset of a horny teenager—where would you go in your building to try and reach hitherto unknown bases? Chances are that anywhere that'd offer some shelter for a bit of under-bra action should also be a prime napping location. Admittedly none of the following locations would score terribly high reviews on TripAdvisor but needs must:

1. DISABLED BATHROOM Yes the thought of laying on the floor of any bathroom that's not your own is somewhat unpalatable, but if you're sick enough to consider it you've probably already been kneeling at its altar and, from experience, a laid-out gym towel makes the whole thing a little less revolting.

2. CLEANING CUPBOARD One thing to consider before bedding down among the vacuum cleaners—make sure there aren't the kind of cleaning chemicals in your cupboard to turn your nap into a sleep from which you never wake.

Style Out A Hangover

No entry
to unauthorised personnel
No smoking or naked lights

Keep well ventilated

Caution
Wet floor

If you're reading this in the office (and we do hope you are, because much like hangovers, poos, and personal admin, catching up on your literature is better done on work time), then take a look to your right and or left at the colleagues in closest proximity to you.

How do they look? A general sense of ennui combined with a gray pallor? That's ok. Heavy-lidded and slumped so far forward that you're not entirely sure of their level of consciousness? Also fine. Bulging veins at their temples, a redness about their face that you'd describe as pre-heart attack, and a jaw clenched so tightly that you're querying tetanus? We hate to break it to you but you might just be a terrible desk buddy who is driving your poor colleagues into a perennial state of fury.

THE SIGNS

Here are some crimes you may unknowingly be committing. If you're guilty of more than three... well we're surprised you're still alive.

1. UNNECESSARY NOISE You probably think you make an average amount of noise, right? The occasional drumming of fingers on your desk when you're concentrating, the odd throat-clearing demi-cough here and there, an infrequent hum when you've got your earphones in and your fave song comes on? Well think again. What barely registers as anything audible to you is registering at environmental health reportable levels to your nearest and (un)dearest.

As a postscript, if you hate those that sit next to you and really want to upset your neighbors, then opt for the most evil desk crime of all—the persistent sniff. Tantamount to waterboarding your poor desk sharers with your own mucus, there is no sound more repulsive than constant snot swallowing.

Be A Good
Desk Buddy

2. REPEATED CONVERSATIONS ABOUT YOUR COMMUTE If you're the kind of person who spends the first 15 minutes of each day detailing the exact duration of the bus delay, retelling the word-for-word conversation you had with the person behind the train ticket counter, or giving a blow-by-blow account of the bumper-to-bumper traffic you encountered on the way, we're going to let you in on a little secret. NO ONE GIVES A SHIT ABOUT YOUR COMMUTE! And they all secretly suspect you're making up the trespasser on the tracks/traffic-inducing protest march/fatal heart attack on your bus because you're late for the third day in a row.

3. OVERLY LOUD TYPING Unless you work in a typing pool, which as it's not the 1950s you probably don't, there's no reason for any ears, apart from maybe your own, to hear the sound of your sausage fingers bashing furiously against your computer keyboard. You might think it makes you seem terribly busy and efficient hammering away like you're trying to punch through sheet metal but it doesn't—it just makes you very annoying.

4. WACKY RING TONES So downloading that Avicii song as your ringtone seemed like a hilarious piece of banter when you were on your hols, but that was eight months ago now and you've kind of forgotten how to change it, so every time you leave your desk and your mom/network provider/lunatic ex calls your colleagues are treated to a tinny 45 seconds of shit euro-dance. Pop it on silent for everyone's sake, hey?

5. USING SPEAKER PHONE Because you're super-super busy why should making a phone call take up all your faculties? Hey, you might have to engage your mouth but let's not tie up a valuable limb while chatting, pop it on speaker and you have both arms free to get on with really important stuff, such as scouring eBay for new listings and finding out which reality star did indeed wear the dress best. Who cares that it means everyone has to endure both sides of your tedious conversation. You're getting shit done!

6. AT-DESK GROOMING No we're not talking about going all Gary Glitter here, but it's almost on a par in levels of hideousness. We mean anything you do to your body that causes it to shed or smell. Think there's no way you'd do anything that gross? Let's see how many you can check off:

• Filing/clipping nails at desk (added vom points for using communal office scissors)

• Vigorous hair brushing to leave behind the kind of forensic evidence that'd wrap up *CSI: Miami* in seconds

• Nail polish removal or application, thus transforming the average office cubicle into a high-school chemistry fume cabinet.

• Perfume/deodorant application—to you it might be delightful but to your colleagues it's on a par with living down the road from a nuclear plant.

8. CONSTANT SNACKING We get it, work can be exceptionally dull and enjoying the odd treat here and there can offer a welcome distraction from the drudgery. However, do we have to endure the sight of you constantly shoveling doughnuts into your gob and the smell of your cola-and-candy-scented burps every single minute of every single day?

Be A Good
Desk Buddy

From what everyone earns to who's really shagging whom, the person who has knowledge also has power. This is why the ability to find out everything about your office is invaluable. Below are the skills you need to perfect:

THE SLY SCREEN SPY

If you're fond of a discreet leer down the front of a blouse, you've got a head start on this one. Basically, you need to train yourself to read someone else's screen, picking up on anything juicy in a fraction of a second without them noticing you've missed a beat when talking to them. It might sound impossible but if you already have in mind the words you're looking for—pay rise, redundancy, STI, criminal embezzlement, etc.—then these words will stand out to you. The same goes for your own name or those of your close colleagues. Words you're familiar with are way easier to recognize, so maybe think about getting some flashcards printed with phrases such as "highly confidential" and "extremely personal" on. Also practice reading as you walk and, if necessary, invest in some strong glasses to buy a few seconds of screen-reading time on the approach to your victim's computer.

MAKE FRIENDS WITH THE OFFICE ADMINISTRATOR

We don't know why terrorist groups throughout the world insist on still using such time-wasting, inconvenient, labor-intensive methods of extracting the truth from people when there is white wine in the world. Why bother with waterboarding when a bottle and a half of self-administered Pinot Grigio will do the same job without any of the unpleasantness. Just as loose lips sink ships, they also reveal just how much of a bonus your loathed boss got at Christmas, the fact that your CEO's been sleeping in his office, and who's top of the list for the next round of redundancies. It's going to take a small initial financial outlay but luckily there's a handy algorithm concerning cheapness of wine and speed in which it renders someone incapable of keeping a secret. Identify your gatekeeper of all such knowledge and test it out.

HANG OUT AROUND THE PHOTOCOPIER

Find Out Anything

You know how if you go to the supermarket at the end of the day you'll be able to snap up a shop-soiled microwave meal for next to nothing? Well a similar phenomenon happens at the end of the day with your office printer. Before the cleaner comes round and chucks away all the printouts your lazy colleagues forgot to go and collect, scoop them up and retreat somewhere quiet for a quick flick through. Long is the juicy list of salaries/disciplinary records or draft resignation letters that have been uncovered this way.

Unfortunately, when it comes to work no man (or woman) is an island. Despite the fact that the idea of enduring some highly invasive keyhole surgery appeals to you more than the thought of having to spend a single extra second with your co-workers once the clock hits 5.30pm, it does pay dividends to cultivate a few friendships in the office.

WHY?

You might think you can't be bothered with work friends. Maybe that's because you're a total recluse and you'd rather eat your sandwiches in the bathroom than have to face the horror of talking to your colleagues. If that's the case, you might as well stop reading now. However, if it's more of a "well I've got enough mates and they're all a bit weird at work," then you need to change your 'tude. Work friends rule. Here's why:

• You don't have to interrupt your bitching about colleagues every two minutes to explain who's who.

• You don't have to make any effort to see them—no trekking out in the rain on a Saturday night for their dog's bat mitzvah or having to get dressed on a Sunday for a bullshit brunch.

• They'll tell you that you have half of your lunch stuck in your teeth.

• They can check if your office crush really is fit or just FFW (see pages 30–33).

• If you have a bad haircut they won't let the office laugh at you.

• You won't have to eat lunch in the bathroom (see above).

• They'll tell you if there are rumors about you and the dodgy bloke in IT

• If you forget your purse/wallet, you won't have to starve all day.

• If you're a girl, who else are you going to hit upon when ladies' day catches you out?

Make Friends And
Influence People

HOW NOT TO MAKE FRIENDS

You'd think people would learn these things at kindergarten, but the workplace does require some different anti-skills:

SAY IT'S NOT MY JOB Nobody likes a jobsworth, and what's the odd extra task here or there if it means you can rely on them for tampons/someone to contribute to your birthday collection/covering for your hangover 'til redundancy do part.

BE A (UNINTENTIONAL) DICK TO COLLEAGUES You could be being annoying without even realizing (see pages 94–97 on how to be a good desk buddy).

BE AN OUT-AND-OUT DICKHEAD TO COLLEAGUES Pretty self-explanatory.

REFUSE TO SIGN BIRTHDAY CARDS Be sneaky, you can skip the contribution when no one's looking but make sure you write something that suggests you were generous.

HAVE AN ANNOYING VOICE Baby or whiny = zero tolerance.

BE TOO MUCH OF A NEGATIVE NANCY OR A POSITIVE PERCY Nobody wants someone that moans all the time but, in an office apocalypse, it'd be the relentlessly upbeat we'd kill first.

HOW TO GET POPULAR

Oh for the days when a rumor that you went to third base and had parents who often went away was all you needed to be Queen or King Bee. It hasn't all completely changed, though, as the below list demonstrates:

BE IN CHARGE OF SOMETHING Identify something that affects every single person in your office. From coffee brand choices to a full-blown office move, if you have the power to make someone's life a whole lot better or a whole lot worse, then they'll be sucking up to you for months.

SMALL TALK We've already covered the fact it's HIDEOUS. But five minutes of listening about how triathlons have absolutely turned Pam's life around after her divorce may give you a lifetime of her sharing her delicious homemade cookies with you.

SHOWER It's that simple.

BRIBE THEM What are your
colleagues' weaknesses? Work out
the ones that are:
a) legal—we're not suggesting you
start cooking up crystal meth in a bid
for buds.
b) aren't going to take too much
effort on your part—think around the
rice krispie cake level of effort.
c) will make others jealous. Booze or
food is a surefire hit unless you work
in a rehab clinic/Weight Watchers
HQ/Amish community.

START A RUMOR How much more
appealing do you think you might be
if your nephew was a member of
One Direction or Richard Branson
was your godfather. Ok, that might be
a little ambitious but sow the seeds
that maybe your dad has a holiday
home in Europe, or your sister works
as an editor for a fashion magazine
and gets loads of beauty products
for free, and watch the friends come
flowing. Will they be genuine?
Unlikely. Do you care? I refer you to
my last answer.

You might think the term "survive" seems a little excessive, but in the February of 2015 a Chinese drug official died after excessive drinking during a work lunch. Now that is extreme but if you want to get through an alcohol-fueled afternoon without getting fired/getting off with your client/getting sick, you'll need to approach it carefully.

THE KEY TO SUCCESS

Follow these tips and you'll soon be able to handle your booze like a 1960's New York ad exec on a mission to snare a new client.

BREAD IS YOUR LIFE RAFT Think of those doughy little lumps as water wings and take advantage of them at every point possible. They will stop you drowning. Eat one before you even sit down. You need something, anything, to hit your stomach before even a drop of that first pre-prandial lands, because if you pour it straight into your nothing-since-breakfast tummy there's no coming back.

ARRIVE EARLY ENOUGH TO CHOOSE YOUR SEAT All manner of things become more prominent after seven or so glasses of paid-for-by-the-company wine, so if you turn up late and end up sitting next to the pervy client/person who's going through a break-up/office stinker you're going to be groped, bored, and nauseous, all before your first course.

FAKE IT When is a drink not a drink? No one but you needs to know. Every couple of drinks throw in a ringer—try tonic with a slice of lemon (no one will know its not stacked with gin), OJ minus the vodka, a convincing-looking mocktail or, at a push, a strong shandy.

BEFRIEND THE WAITER If he's your mate he won't announce to the table that he's looking for the person that ordered the NON-ALCOHOLIC LAGER or VIRGIN MARY, plus he can be bribed into topping everyone else's glasses up while deftly skipping over yours.

ALARM YOURSELF Put your phone to vibrate and set an alarm that goes off every half an hour or so. Each time that happens a) drink a glass of water b) take yourself off to the bathroom to have a little word with yourself and an appraisal of your level of drunkenness.

KNOWING WHEN TO QUIT

If any of the following happen GO HOME:

**Survive
A Boozy Lunch**

• You see a hand creeping onto your crotch (and it's not just yours that you've lost feeling in due to being so drunk).

• You start to fancy anyone and everyone round the table.

• Someone suggests a game of beer pong, and you're in a Michelin-starred restaurant.

• You've thrown up a little in your mouth.

• You go and ask the DJ to play some Miley Cyrus. Except it's not a DJ, it's your own reflection in a mirror and it's 3 in the afternoon.

• Someone pees somewhere that isn't a toilet.

• You let your boss have a go on your Tinder.

• The company credit card has gone missing.

• You start crying.

• You feel tempted to tell your boss the "real" truth about what everyone thinks of her.

CHAPTER 4
THE EVENTS

In these cash-strapped times, when it comes to Christmas parties the only real fun to be had is in discussing dos thrown by those mystical, still-have-cash companies. The kind of party where there's a free bar, partners are allowed, and a "singer" who came ninth in *The X Factor* performs, have become urban legend. Everyone's heard of one. Your cousin's dog groomer's plumber had last year's knees-up in a posh hotel with a suite for each employee. You've seen the pictures on Facebook. You think...

For the rest of us it's Doritos, sweaty cheese, and cheap wine in plastic cups served in a hastily cleared conference room, soundtracked by someone's iPod handily dropped into one of the aforementioned plastic cups. "It makes a good speaker," according to the IT man. Yes it does... if you happen to be an ant with exquisite aural skills. Having said that, not being able to hear Mariah Carey punctuated with adverts for Anusol (because everyone's been too tight to fork out for Spotify Premium) isn't too much of a hardship. So far, so terrible, right? But don't panic. You can get through it, simply pick a desired outcome and follow these key points:

AIM: **TO PULL THE OFFICE HOTTIE**

DO: Splash a little bit of cash (if you can expense it, even better). Turning up with a snazzy bottle of champers (prosecco will do) under your arm to a party where, gallon for gallon, petrol would cost more than the provided wine (and probably taste better) guarantees attention from the whole room. It's a trick reminiscent of teenage house parties but guess what—it still works. Use a glass of bubbly to rescue your crush from a night of esophageal torture caused by ingesting vinegary plonk, then hint that there's plenty more where that came from. They'll be putty in your hands.

DON'T: Ply them with too much booze. No one wants a sexual harassment charge on their disciplinary record.

AIM: **TO BEFRIEND THE BOSS**

DO: Research your target. Don't put your foot in it by asking about the wife and kids when he's recently left them to shack up with his one-time PA, or has just been dumped in favor of a 25-year-old personal trainer. Proving difficult to find this info? Take a good look at the man. Is he sporting a beard that verges on neglect? Are his shirts suddenly as crumpled as Hugh Hefner's bedding? She's left him. Penis-extension Porsche in the office car park and Gucci belt suddenly holding up his paunch? He's snared himself what your mother would call a dolly bird.

The Christmas Party

DON'T: Think eight drinks in is the right time to tell him your thoughts on how to run the company. You'll only end up petitioning for the right to glory holes in the bathrooms or corporal punishment for stapler thieves.

AIM: TO DRINK THROUGH THE PAIN

DO: Pre-game. For total and complete oblivion there's probably not going to be enough booze at your carefully-budgeted-per-head event. Loosen yourself up with something socially acceptable like Buck's Fizz from around mid-afternoon. No one needs to know the ratio of orange juice to fizz is akin to your chance of winning the lottery.

DON'T: Arrive late. The good (i.e. strong) drinks will be served first and will as such run out first. Welcome cocktails are your friend. Take as many as you can and then secret them away in a hiding place (this hiding place may well be your stomach).

AIM: TO GAIN BLACKMAILABLE MATERIAL

DO: Fake your boozing. You want to give the impression of being as wasted as everyone else while you remain fully alert to office indiscretions. Helpful hints to this include: **a)** tying your tie around your head in the manner of a Rambo-esque character, AKA the public schoolboy at a wedding **b)** untucking one side of your shirt or taking off your high heels and staggering everywhere in your stockinged feet.

If you're combining this aim with befriending the boss and he or she is of the opposite sex you may also introduce a "hilarious" party game at this point. Something with balloons and body contact usually works and will probably be an easy gateway into the kind of hedonism usually seen only at WASP swingers parties.

DON'T: Let your phone battery die. You know the rules, pictures or it didn't happen.

The Christmas Party

There's little to thank the general economic slowdown of the world for, but the fact that it's severely diminished the amount of "fun" away days a company can afford to enforce upon you is something that you should give thanks for. Funnily enough the world still turns and work still gets done without identifying whether Dave is a natural-born leader in a survival situation, or knowing that Jackie feels uninhibited about expressing her feelings through the medium of a mime.

To the naively initiated a day out of the office sounds like a good thing but read on, and you'll soon change your mind...

THE PHYSICAL ONE

AKA BUILDING A BLOODY RAFT

What is it about the task of building some kind of makeshift boat with 14 of your colleagues that makes it in any way useful to your working life? Unless you're a lifeguard/work on a cruise ship/are Bear Grylls, it's unlikely you're ever going to need to quickly pull together some kind of life-saving flotation device and, if you did, you'd probably just save yourself to be honest. In a life or death situation Janice and Roy from the complaint department, who you have spoken to maybe twice in four years, can sort themselves out.

If you're based a prohibitive distance away from a suitable water source your boss might have to think outside the raft box. Sadly all that lies outside is an endless realm of assault courses, zip wiring through trees, trembling your way up a rope ladder, and crawling through muck and mire under the watchful eye of some overweight former security guard who's lied about having a military background.

The Team Building Day

THE HUMILIATING ONE

AKA THE ONE WITH ENFORCED NUDITY

Whether it's something that involves a swimsuit or even worse something that doesn't (you may laugh but massages/saunas/hammams that involve no kit whatsoever are all documented examples of someone's idea of a bonding exercise), no good can come of having a clear picture of what your colleagues look like naked. A lose/lose situation; if they're hot, you won't be able to stop daydreaming and if they're not... well you'll never be able to look them in the eye again (although god knows where else you'll look).

THE SWANKY ONE

AKA THE ONE YOU'RE NEVER INVITED TO

Beyond all the sweat, dirt, running underneath disused parachutes, and creating human Venn diagrams there does exist the holy grail of away days. It is the overnighter in a luxury country hotel complete with three-course gourmet meal, semi-famous after-dinner speaker, and UNLIMITED FREE BAR! The bad news? The nearest you're going to get to this is via a social media slip up when one of your high-ranking executives goes a little too wild with the complimentary Cab Sav and forgets about the unspoken rule of not allowing the proletariat to see where their Christmas party fund is really being spent.

THE HIPPY DIPPY ONE

AKA THE ONE WHERE YOU'LL HAVE TO SIT ON THE FLOOR ALL DAY

From dancing out your feelings to finding your spirit animal, it's a "no shoes, no shame" kinda environment. Led by someone who has taken their name from an element of nature, never owned a nail brush, and dresses entirely from Woodstock's lost property box, expect one co-worker to get really into it and spend half the day sobbing as the "write your goals as a haiku to your inner child" class releases a deep-seated memory about the time they got given the red not the blue sippy cup at nursery. Handily this will mean Storm has to roll up his sleeves (revealing a myriad of gap year friendship bracelets) and take care of them, thus releasing the rest of you to search around for his recreational drugs stash.

The Team Building Day

THE DANGEROUS ONE

AKA THE ONE WHERE YOU HAVE TO PRETEND YOU TRUST YOUR COLLEAGUES

Frankly you wouldn't give that bitch in graphic design your computer password and you fudged your address when you had to fill out a gift-aid form to sponsor the creep IT guy to run a half marathon, so it's fair to say you would rather not put your life in the hands of the various imbeciles that haunt your working hours. But that's exactly what you'll be expected to do on the trust-building day. From the verging on sexual assault "led through a maze blindfolded" to the you now owe me three months worth of spinal care "falling back from height into the hands of your team," the only upside of all of this is you might come out of it with a way to sue your boss.

Nine-to-five in one room, with the same people, and only a sandwich platter to break up the boredom, when it comes to the all-dayer, there's only one aim: Must. Not. Fall. Asleep. It's easier said than done when breathing in the same recycled air and listening to the same monotonous voices with the light dimming for yet another Powerpoint presentation. It's as narcolepsy-inducing as seven hours of subtitled arthouse cinema. Getting though this alive (and awake) means you're going to have to find ways of amusing yourself.

MEETING BINGO

Does Paul clear his throat a little before every monologue? Does Amy pepper her sentences with more "likes" than Dan Bilzerian's Instagram feed? Maybe Sam makes a funny gesture with his hands every time he tries to make a point or Ellie has a habit of adjusting her ponytail when she's concentrating? Whatever your colleagues' irritating foibles, stop them driving you to slowly and inefficiently murder them by hole punch by turning their habits into a bingo game. Reward yourself for a full house with a pretend trip to the bathroom where you can have a whole five minutes of me time.

GET APPY

Technology, you have blighted our workplace in many ways but when it comes to boredom we really do owe you. No one takes a notebook into meetings any more, right? Instead, you sit smugly "taking notes" on your iPad. Sounds like an easy win, right? Don't be foolish enough to think you'll be able to kick back and watch subtitled Netflix or text a blow-by-blow account of last night's date to a friend; that's way too noticeable. Instead, you'll need to find something that doesn't involve you typing constantly, or not typing at all, and also gives you periods of reflection to look like you're concentrating. Think a crossword app, Words With Friends, or, at a push, a backlog of BuzzFeed quizzes. That should trick 'em.

SNOG, MARRY, AVOID

They (whoever "they" are) say that a good way to quell nerves is to imagine your audience naked. Well it also kind of works when you're extremely bored. Admittedly, it's a bit creepy to be lingering too long over what might be lurking under that nylon blouse or ill-fitting suit, so try a more PG-friendly version and force yourself to decide who'd get the tongue, the ring, and the brush off. The grosser your colleagues, the more entertaining.

The All-day Meeting

GO OLD SCHOOL

What did you do when you were bored in class at school? Try and set the meeting off course. Think of it as the work day version of calling out "teacher, teacher" every couple of minutes and constantly ask for points to be clarified, objectives to be spelt out, and a little more time to really make sure you note that last idea down. Yes everyone else will hate you but it'll keep you conscious.

BECOME A PEN MAJORETTE

Think of your biro as a baton and see what gymnastic feats you can perform with it. You'll have perfected a double-handed spin roll in no time.

THEME IT

Give everyone in the meeting a theme tune. The fat one gets some kind of tuba solo, the creepy one something screechy and irregular, the nice-but-dim one some kind of Disney medley, the hateful one something scary and religious.

CAST AWAY

Who would play each of your colleagues in a film? The crueller the comparison, the better, so expect lots of upcoming roles for Roseanne Barr/Zach Galifianakis/Steve Buscemi/Rosie O'Donnell.

COUNTDOWN

Count anything and everything you can see. Carpet tiles, letter E's in the meeting notes, the amount of times the creep next to you plays pocket billiards, the remaining hairs on your balding colleague's head. All will buy you precious seconds of wakefulness.

GIRLS ONLY

Do your kegels. Boys, don't look this up, you won't like it.

PUSH YOUR BODY

See how long you can hold your breath for (added points if you pass out and the meeting has to stop); see how many seconds you can stare at something without blinking (maybe your most loathed colleague in the room to freak them out); try and remain totally immobile for a set period of time (it's a lot shorter than you think); or see how many cookies you can force down before you throw up.

The All-day Meeting

For reasons unknown, when given a little bit of corporate responsibility some people completely lose the ability to speak in clear, comprehensible terms—they talk nonsense, basically. Sadly, this condition is infecting employees in offices across the globe. You may even work with such a person. Here are some translations to help you decipher the BS they spout:

REACH OUT

Sadly, this is not a specialist sex move. Instead, it's a way for people that you never wanted to hear from in the first place to dress up their irritating reason for getting in touch as something more exciting. "I just thought I'd reach out to find out what you're working on at the moment." Well reach back in, please.

TIMEBOX

"Let's timebox that report." Yeah, because everyone hates a deadline, don't they? Deadlines just sound so doom and gloom and worky! Let's give it a snappy title like "timebox" instead and then no one's going to mind the fact they've got to work an 80-hour week to keep to it because it'll feel like fun!

STAND-UP: LET'S HAVE A

Apparently, this is now a name for a meeting you don't sit down for, or have in a meeting room. So a conversation then.

YOU SAY THAT THEN?

The Glossary

HUDDLE: LETS HAVE A

Much the same as a stand-up, but closer. And creepier.

360 VIEW

As opposed to what? Shutting one eye and giving ourselves a 180?

ON MY RADAR

Sorry, we thought you were in middle management. We must have missed the part where you had a career change to submarine pilot.

FLIGHT PLAN

So you're not only a submarine pilot but also a regular airplane one, too!

LOW-HANGING FRUIT

Not your granny's wartime slang for a promiscuous homosexual.

PUT A RECORD ON AND SEE WHO DANCES

Are you a DJ?

GOING FORWARD

Could you go forward quite quickly in that direction please. Yes, that way with the cliff and the 50-foot drop.

REAL TIME

Well we weren't planning on calculating the deadline in terms of the axial tilt of Mars, we were going to go ahead and use the regular Gregorian calendar, too.

OPEN DOOR POLICY

What about when it closes? All doors have the ability to do this you know. Unless they're broken. Maybe it should be called a broken door policy, instead.

TAKE IT TO THE NEXT LEVEL

What do you mean by that exactly. Should I whizz into the lift and read you the report from the floor above? Would that make it make more sense?

CHECK FOR ALLERGIC REACTIONS

Hearing this phrase is, ironically, enough to make you red, breathless, and erratic of heart rate. But there's no need to reach for the anti-histamines— this is just a "humorous" way of suggesting you work out what problems there might be before embarking on a project.

BEST PRACTICE

A total bullshit phrase that means nothing at all but can be pulled out by anyone to back up any bullshit argument. It's a mythical state of affairs, practiced in a mythical land, and can cover the most minor "You think we should upgrade the coffee to brand not supermarket own? That's not best practice I'm afraid," to the thunderingly major "No I'm afraid you can't have more than a week off even if your entire family has been torched in an alien fireball attack, it's simply not best practice."

STAFF ENGAGEMENT

This has nothing to do with toilets or Tiffany rings.

WORKFLOW

AKA how work is done. AKA work.

TEMPERATURE CHECK

Unfortunately nothing to do with inserting anything into the rectum of the idiot that first thought this was a good way of saying "Let's take an overall look."

LOOK UNDER THE BONNET

Do you work in a garage?

DON'T LET THE GRASS GROW TOO LONG

Do you work on a tennis court?

PUSH BACK

What sounds like an American Football move is, in fact, a pass-agg way of saying "That's not good enough."

CLOSE OF PLAY

Always said by men who consider being able to throw a scrunched-up piece of paper successfully into the bin across the room as a major aphrodisiac.

LET'S WORKSHOP THAT

Let's not.

TO PARK A PROJECT

Are you a driving instructor?

HELICOPTER VIEW

Since when did you get a pilot's license?

WE SHOULD CONNECT

If you use this phrase we probably shouldn't.

IDEAS SHOWER

AKA the new brainstorm. Apparently, brainstorm was offensive to epileptics (said no epileptics ever) so we have to have thoughts raining down on our heads instead of kicking about inside of them.

RAISE IT UP THE FLAGPOLE AND SEE WHICH WAY IT FLUTTERS

Couldn't we just ask people for their opinion? This way seems like a terrible faff.

NO I IN TEAM

But there is a U in "See you next Tuesday."

SQUARE THE CIRCLE

Physically impossible. Even one-year-old children know the square shape doesn't go in the round hole.

PING

You will not ping me an email. Presumably this comes from the annoying ping that nobody has left to sound on their computers to signify an incoming email since *Sleepless in Seattle*. Are we four? Do we need to describe everything with onomatopoeia?

CASCADE THE INFORMATION

To tell the people around you stuff. Or talk.

I'd like to say thank you to all my wonderful colleagues over the years, this book would not have been possible without you.

Thanks also to everyone at Dog 'n' Bone, Paul Tilby for the design, Emma Hill for editing, and Paul Parker for illustrating.

The publisher would like to thank Caroline West for her help at proof stage.